Helion & Company Limited
Unit 8 Amherst Business Centre
Budbrooke Road
Warwick
CV34 5WE
England
Tel. 01926 499 619
Email: info@helion.co.uk
Website: www.helion.co.uk
Twitter: @helionbooks
Visit our blog https://helionbooks.wordpress.com/

Typeset by Oliver Barstow, Milan, Italy
Cover design by Paul Hewitt, Battlefield Design (www.battlefield-design.co.uk)

ISBN 978-1-804510-31-5

British Library Cataloguing-in-Publication Data
A catalogue record for this book is available from the British Library

CONTENTS

I0893647

Note: In order to simplify the use of this book, all names, locations and geographic designations are as provided in *The Times World Atlas*, or other traditionally accepted major sources of reference, as of the time of described events.

ACRONYMS AND ABBREVIATIONS

AB	Air Base
AD	*Acción Democrática* (Democratic Action) (political party)
ARMA	*Alianza Revolucionaria de Militares Activos* (Revolutionary Alliance of Active Military) (political movement within the Venezuelan armed forces)
ARV	*Armada de la República de Venezuela* (Navy of the Republic of Venezuela)
Copei	*Comité de Organización Política Electoral Independiente* (Independent Committee for Electoral Political Organisation)
DAAFAR	*Defensa Anti-Aérea y Fuerza Aérea Revolucionaria* (Anti-Aircraft Defence Revolutionary Air Force) (Cuba)
DIM	*Dirección de Inteligencia Militar* (Directorate of Military Intelligence)
DISIP	*Dirección de los Servicios de Inteligencia y Prevención* (National Directorate of Intelligence and Prevention Services)
DSN	*Dirección de Suguridad Nacional* (Directorate of National Security) (secret police service)
EAM	*Escuela de Aviación Militar* (Military Aviation School)
FALN	*Fuerzas Armadas de Liberación Nacional* (Armed Forces of National Liberation) (armed insurgency)
FAN	*Fuerzas Armadas Nacionales* (National Armed Forces)
FAV	*Fuerza Aérea Venezolana* (Venezuelan Air Force)
MBR-200	*Movimiento Bolivariano Revolucionario-200* (Revolutionary Bolivarian Movement-200)
MIR	*Movimiento de Izquierda Revolucionaria* (Revolutionary Left Movement) (political movement)
PCV	*Partido Comunista de Venezuela* (*Communist* Party of Venezuela) (political party)
PRV	*Partido de la Revolución Venezolana* (Party of the Venezuelan Revolution)
R83	*Revolución 1983* (political movement within the Venezuelan armed forces)
URD	*Union Republicana Democrática* (Democratic Republican Union) (political party)

AN EDITORIAL NOTE

You currently hold in your hand, in physical or electronic format, the first volume of José Daniel Fernández Dugarte's dynamic account of the 1992 coup attempts in Venezuela. When the editorial team at Helion received José's manuscript we came to realise that it was, unfortunately, too long to accommodate in a single volume using the @War format. Furthermore, without radically restructuring José's work, there was not an easy method by which we could recount the complete events of the first coup of 1992 in the first volume and the events of the second coup attempt in the second volume without producing two very unbalanced volumes in terms of word and page count, or drastically cutting away much of the background and history of the Venezuelan armed forces. We have therefore taken the decision to partition this volume part-way through the events of the first coup attempt following the chapter structure of José's manuscript. We recognise that this leaves the reader with something of a cliff-hanger ending to this volume and hope that you will understand this decision and pick up the story and discover the conclusion presented in Volume 2.

PREFACE

> *...Compañeros, lamentablemente, por ahora, los objetivos que nos planteamos no fueron logrados en la ciudad capital. Es decir, nosotros acá en Caracas no logramos controlar el poder ...*
> (Comrades, unfortunately, for now, the objectives that we have set ourselves could not be accomplished in the capital city. This means that we, here in Caracas, were unable to attain power...)

The above words are from a TV broadcast by a still-unknown Lieutenant Colonel Hugo Chávez, who shortly before midnight had launched a coup d'état attempt that resulted in failure. They day was 4 February 1992, and for the first time in almost 30 years, the Venezuelan people had witnessed a military uprising.

It would not be long until another rebellion took place. Later that year, on 27 November, another uprising occurred. This time, besides toppling the government, the rebels, now supported by a faction of the Air Force, sought to free Chávez from the prison where he was being held.

To understand how the country found itself in a situation where hundreds of soldiers were shooting at each other in the streets of its most populous cities, with the Air Force divided and performing spectacular bombing raids and dogfights, leaving hundreds of casualties, we must look back to the guerrilla movements that were active during the 1960s and 1970s since the ideological influence of these groups founded some of the basis for the 1992 uprisings. Also, the previous military uprisings that had occurred three decades before left some lessons that the rebels used on 4 February and 27 November, influencing the preparation, objective-setting and development of the rebellions.

'(...) Y VENEZUELA SIEMPRE SERÁ UN CUARTEL'

Simón José Antonio de la Santísima Trinidad Bolívar Ponte y Palacios Blanco, commonly known simply as Simón Bolívar, the man who led Venezuelan troops during the bloody Independence War that took place between 1810 and 1823, once said that 'Ecuador will always be a convent; Colombia will always be a university; and Venezuela will always be a barrack'. The latter description, albeit simplistic, has proven true historically.

Looking back to the origin of the Venezuelan nation, its history has been characterised by a fondness for militaristic rulers that is somewhat common in Latin America, which is itself a land of *Caudillos*.[1]

Between 1830, the year in which Venezuela regained its independence from Colombia, and 1903, when the last rebel troops under command of Nicolás Rolando Monteverde and Manuel Antonio Matos were defeated in the Battle of Ciudad Bolívar, marking the end of the *Revolución Libertadora* (the Liberating Revolution), the country experienced a generalised state of lawlessness, civil war and *caudillismo* that left it as one of the poorest countries in the world by the time the situation was stabilised under the rule of General José Cipriano Castro Ruiz, a *caudillo* himself.

By late-1902, peace was already in sight as the government troops advanced in their fight against the rebels. At the time, the country was heavily indebted due to the damage suffered by properties belonging to foreigners, especially Europeans, during the turmoil of the previous century. When the Venezuelan government failed to honour this debt, a naval blockade was imposed on the country by the United Kingdom, Germany and Italy; an event which we will discuss as we delve deeper into the history of the country.

With an increased influence of the United States in Latin America, tensions started to arise between Caracas and Washington, with Castro's nationalist views opposing the American meddling in Venezuela's internal issues. Eventually, in 1908, shortly after Castro's ship sailed for France for him to receive medical treatment, an American-supported bloodless coup was staged by his aide and second-in-command, General Juan Vicente Gómez Chacón.

Gómez, who adopted the title of *El Benemérito* (the distinguished, or meritorious), ruled with an iron fist until his death on 17 December 1935, handing power to three of his associates for short periods through his tenure; José Gil Fortul, from 1913 to 1914; Victorino Márquez Bustillos, from 1914 to 1922; and Juan Bautista Pérez, from 1929 to 1931. Even though they were nominally presidents, it was Gómez who ultimately held the most power in the country. It was during his rule that oil was first extracted for commercial purposes in the western state of Zulia. This marked the beginning of a new era for Venezuela; one characterised by considerable oil revenues, investment in public works, development of urban centres and militarism.

With *El Benemérito*'s passing in 1935, another general, José Eleazar López Contreras, succeeded him. A reformist, López Contreras rapidly disbanded Gómez's security apparatus and

Simón Bolívar (1783–1830), one of the principal architects of the independence of Bolivia, Colombia, Ecuador, Panama, Peru, and Venezuela. (National Art Gallery of Caracas)

José Cipriano Castro Ruiz, a high-ranking officer of the Venezuelan armed forces, and the President of Venezuela from 1899 to 1908. (*Presidencia de la República de Venezuela*)

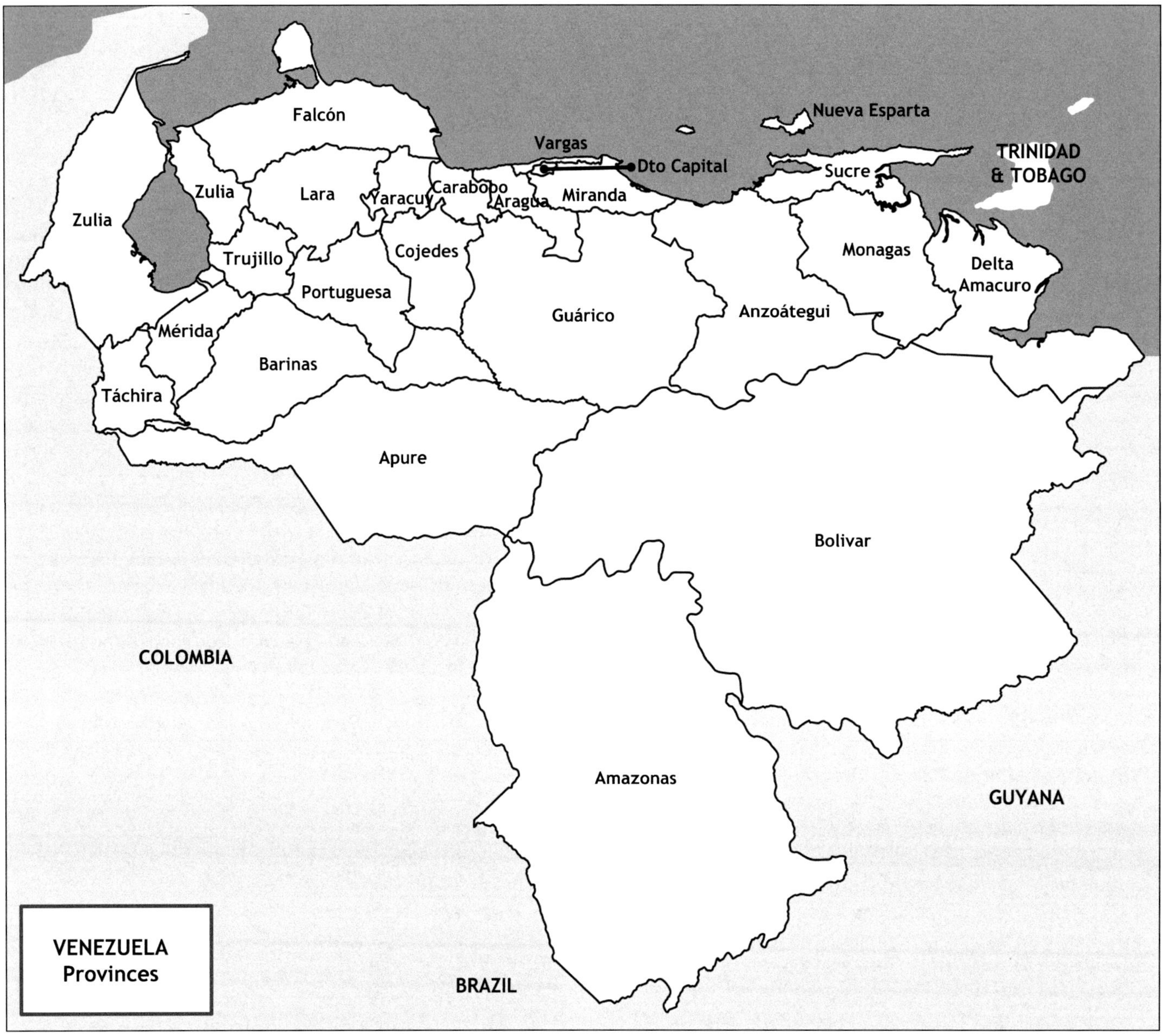

Map of Venezuela and its states. (Map by Tom Cooper)

freed political prisoners. He also aimed for greater flexibility in the political dynamics of Venezuela, allowing for a limited separation of powers and allowing the *Congreso Nacional* (the Parliament), to act freely within a definite frame of autonomy that it did not enjoy during his predecessor's tenure.

López Contreras was replaced in 1941 by General Isaías Medina Angarita after a voting in the *Congreso*. Medina Angarita, who had been Minister of War under López Contreras, was often accused of being sympathetic to fascism. However, he maintained Venezuela as a neutral party through most of the Second World War, even though Venezuelan-flagged tanker ships were sunk in the Caribbean Sea during Operation *Neuland*. He ultimately sealed his compromise with the Allies when he became the first president of Venezuela to travel abroad while in office, visiting the Bolivarian countries in 1942 and 1943,[2] and the United States in 1944, where he met President Franklin Delano Roosevelt.

Medina Angarita was supposed to remain in power until at least 1946, when a new vote in the Parliament was to decide who would succeed him or if he would rule for another term. However, on 18 October 1945, a successful coup staged by *Acción Democrática* (AD, Democratic Action) ousted him, marking the end of the *gomecismo*[3] and the beginning of the *Trienio Adeco*.[4] A *junta*, the *Junta Revolucionaria de Gobierno* (Revolutionary Government Junta), composed of seven members (five civilians and two military officers), and headed by Rómulo Ernesto Betancourt Bello, assumed executive powers.

While the word *Revolucionaria* might suggest some sort of communist leaning, considering the years we are talking about, the *Partido Comunista de Venezuela* (*PCV*, Communist Party of Venezuela) did not have any presence in the government. In fact, it had been legalised only nine days before by Medina Angarita.

During the *junta*'s three-year government, a new Constitution was approved in 1947, replacing the one that had been in force since López Contreras' period in 1936. Among other things, it was the first Venezuelan Constitution that contemplated free and direct elections, as well as allowing females to vote.

This paved the way for what is widely considered as Venezuela's first free and fair election, on 14 December 1947. The winner was Rómulo Ángel del Monte Carmelo Gallegos Freire, a novelist and member of *AD* since its founding. This was not, however, Venezuela's

Rómulo Ernesto Betancourt Bello, president of Venezuela from 1945 to 1948, and again from 1959 to 1964. (*Presidencia de la República de Venezuela*)

Official photograph of General Marcos Pérez Jiménez, who ruled Venezuela as a member of the military *junta* from 1950 to 1952, and as president from 1952 to 1958. (*Presidencia de la República de Venezuela*)

first presidential election. In 1860, Manuel Felipe de Tovar won an election held in a war-torn country. At the time, the Federal War was being fought; a conflict that ultimately cost Venezuela around 10 percent of its population and a heavy toll of infrastructure damage.

Gallegos' presidency was brief, lasting little more than nine months, from 17 February to 24 November 1948. That day, something that had been usual in the previous century happened again: the Army revolted and exiled Gallegos from Venezuela, establishing the *Junta Militar de Gobierno* (Military Government Junta) integrated by Lieutenant Colonel Carlos Román Delgado Chalbaud Gómez, its president; Marcos Evangelista Pérez Jiménez, and Luis Felipe Llovera Páez. One of the first actions of the new government was to derogate the Constitution of 1947.

Officially, the *junta* was to stay in power for a short period, create what they considered ideal conditions for a new free and fair election, and then hand power to whoever the people elected in the process. Negotiations were underway for the voting when, on 13 November 1950, Delgado Chalbaud was kidnapped and murdered by Rafael Simón Urbina López, a crime that remains a matter of controversy to this day.

Theories are many and polemical. It is widely believed, however, that the plot was orchestrated by Pérez Jiménez as he considered Delgado Chalbaud an obstacle in his way to power. Had there been an election, Delgado Chalbaud would have been the candidate supported by the military. If he won, the *junta* would have been dissolved and both Pérez Jiménez and Llovera Páez left aside and most likely relegated to some ministry, ultimately leaving Delgado Chalbaud as the most powerful man in the country. Opposed to this theory is the fact that Pérez Jiménez's wife, Flor María Chalbaud Castro, was Carlos Delgado Chalbaud's cousin.

Delgado Chalbaud was replaced as the *junta*'s head by civilian lawyer Germán Suárez Flamerich, who acted as a façade for Pérez Jiménez. Given that there was no Constitution in force at the time, a direct vote was not a possibility to elect the next leader of Venezuela.

An election for a Constituent Assembly was called for 30 November 1952. Besides drafting a new Constitution, the deputies would elect who would rule the country for the next five years. When the results were announced, it was what most people expected: The *Frente Electoral Independiente* (*FEI*, Independent Electoral Front), Pérez Jiménez's party, largely defeated Jóvito Villalba Gutiérrez's *Unión Republicana Democrática* (*URD*, Democratic Republican Union) with 788,000 votes against 638,000. Allegations of fraud immediately surfaced, claiming that the real result had been 1,198,000 against 403,000 in favour of the *URD*. Regardless of this, Pérez Jiménez claimed victory and expelled Villalba from the country.

The next five years under Marcos Evangelista Pérez Jiménez, who was sworn as president on 2 January 1953, saw the fast development of infrastructure and economic growth, all fuelled by high oil prices in the early years of the Cold War. Despite the militaristic nature of the regime, the Venezuelan administration was drastically different from other Latin American governments of similar characteristics, not being seen as an international pariah, but as the architect of the transformation of a predominantly rural and impoverished country into one of the most prestigious and economically prosperous members of the international community.

Politically, during the period following the 1948 coup, Venezuela aligned itself with the United States, joining its anti-communist efforts in Latin America. In this situation, the *PCV* was declared illegal soon after the military takeover and its members hunted by the secret police, the *Dirección de Seguridad Nacional* (*DSN*,

National Security Directorate). *AD* was also made illegal, having some of its leaders like Antonio Pinto Salinas and Leonardo Ruíz Pineda killed by the *DSN*, and others, like Luis Alberto Carnevali Rangel, dying while in custody under unclear circumstances.

Many members of the opposition, coming from both political parties and dissident sectors within the military, were sent to the concentration camp of Guasina, located in an isolated island in the Orinoco River Delta. On 23 January 1958, a new revolt took place in Venezuela. Pérez Jiménez was forced to flee the country after trying to resist the putschists through the day. As soon as he left, all support for the regime crumbled, except in the *DSN* headquarters, whose members knew that they would be massacred by the masses if they surrendered. Past midnight, on 24 January, the defenders were overrun, and the building set ablaze, with some agents being lynched by the mobs. Behind this new putsch was *AD*, still headed by Rómulo Betancourt, who had been exiled since January 1949. He gathered support from various dissidents living abroad, like Jóvito Villalba and Rafael Antonio Caldera Rodríguez, who would be president later, as well as from some young military officers who wanted a transition to democracy in Venezuela.

After Pérez Jiménez left, there were two brief acting governments, one presided by Admiral Wolfgang Enrique Larrazábal Ugüeto and the second by lawyer Luis Edgar Sanabria Arcia. On 7 December 1958 the first direct presidential election since that of 1947 was held. *AD*'s Betancourt defeated *URD*'s Larrazábal by almost 400,000 votes. Betancourt was sworn in as president on 15 February 1959, marking the beginning of a new era for Venezuela, and earning him the title of *El Padre de la Democracia Venezolana* (The Father of the Venezuelan Democracy) among *AD*'s supporters.

The Venezuelan Bipartisan Experiment

On 31 October 1958 the Puntofijo Pact was signed by three of the four major parties that participated in the ousting of Pérez Jiménez. *AD*, *URD* and Rafael Caldera's *Comité de Organización Política Electoral Independiente* (*Copei*, Independent Political Electoral Organisation Committee) agreed to recognise each other's victories in elections in order to maintain stability and to prevent the military from taking power by force again. The fourth, excluded party that fought against Pérez Jiménez was the *PCV*. Various reasons have been cited for its exclusion, ranging from its opposition to *Copei*'s links with the Catholic Church to its links with the Communist Party of the Soviet Union. In this situation, the communists were effectively expelled from the new Venezuelan political scene despite being a legal party since the rebellion in January. This contributed to a rising resentment towards the three major parties.

Weak support for communism had existed in Latin America since the late 1910s. In a region that has historically suffered from chronic poverty and social inequality, the Marxist ideal had often proven popular among the masses. However, it was not until 1936, when Leon Trotsky landed in Mexico, that organised efforts to bring 'the revolution' to Latin America began.

The *PCV* was established in 1931 and quickly declared illegal by Gómez's government, a measure that was maintained during the tenures of López Contreras and most of that of Medina Angarita. Even though its members were often prosecuted and imprisoned, the party managed to celebrate its First Congress in 1937. It was not until 1945, as mentioned before, that the *PCV* was legalised for three years, having supported Rómulo Gallegos' candidacy for the 1947 election. The following year it was once again made illegal by the military government. During this period, the *PCV* actively participated in rioting and underground syndicate activities, forming a net of supporters that played a key role in the ousting of Pérez Jiménez in 1958.

Carlos Andrés Pérez Rodríguez, President of Venezuela from 1974 to 1979, and from 1989 to 1993. (*Presidencia de la República de Venezuela*))

Before the Cuban Revolution, leftist movements in Latin America had difficulty in receiving material assistance from the Soviet Union, which since the end of Second World War had sponsored and supported armed communist movements elsewhere in the world, as happened in the Greek and Chinese civil wars. After the fall of Havana on 1 January 1959, the Soviets now had a platform to effectively project their power and influence through a continent where their ideas had sympathisers among the local population. In this situation, arms started to flow from Soviet ports to Cuba, and from there, to the rest of Latin America.

Civil wars soon erupted throughout the continent. The first cases were Colombia, which to this day is still suffering the consequences of the conflict; Guatemala, where the war lasted for 36 years and claimed over 150,000 lives; and Venezuela, where the conflict was short-lived and of low intensity through most of its duration.

The leadership in Moscow and Havana knew that to be able to effectively support and finance communist guerrillas in the continent, they first needed to have Venezuela within their sphere of influence. After all, it is the country that possesses the world's biggest oil reserves. Furthermore, it has a privileged location in the north of South America, with a long coast on the Caribbean in the north, and access to the Brazilian and Colombian Amazonian forest in the south, both of which have proven to be perfect environments in which to wage a guerrilla war.

With support from Cuba and the Soviet Union, the *PCV* started an armed insurgency in 1960. The involvement of both countries, however, was not as significant as it was in Central America or Colombia, partly because the government in Havana was aware that their Venezuelan counterparts were willing and able to respond with force if the groups they sponsored became a serious threat to the country's stability. Furthermore, the Venezuelan military was more

An aerial view of the downtown of the booming Caracas in the mid-1970s. (Mark Lepko Collection)

capable than that of other targeted Latin American countries, which meant a bigger investment of resources would have been needed in a situation where the odds were against the revolutionaries.

One of the main goals of the guerrilla campaign from its beginning was to delegitimise the government, something that could only be achieved by provoking low turnouts in the elections. For this, the insurgents resolved to use terror tactics to generate anxiety and panic among the population. However, contrary to what they expected, support for the multiparty system increased, with turnouts for the 1963 and 1968 elections being above 90 percent, delivering a big political defeat to the guerrillas, which was essentially the beginning of the end of their role as a relevant disruptor of the Venezuelan political scene. Through the next two decades, until the late 1980s, the political left fragmented into several minor parties whose influence was effectively negligible, facilitating the dominance by *AD* and *Copei*.

At the same time, within the military, some groups were not content with the new status quo brought by the new regime. Having attained power for most of Venezuela's republican history, they were now relegated to their garrisons and had their political influence reduced to none. The early 1960s was marked by a series of uprisings against Betancourt's government that had different natures, some being supported by the communists, and some having a nationalistic ideology.

Politically, the 1960s in Venezuela can be described as tense, with a strong, but still-in-the-building democratic system threatened by various elements of the national life. Although the insurgent activity was of low intensity and its reach was limited, urban activism proved to be a major problem for the government, with student and worker strikes being commonplace throughout the country. This tension only started to dissipate by the end of the decade, when Rafael Caldera, of *Copei*, was elected president for a five-year term in 1969. For the first time in Venezuelan history, the transition of power between two rival parties was achieved without controversy or violence.

The following years saw a continuation of the development of the country, which was greatly boosted by the oil crisis of 1973. In a short period of time, Venezuela saw its oil revenues multiply by four, with crude barrel prices rising from US$3 to US$12 between 1973 and 1976. In this situation, the government, now headed by Carlos Andrés Pérez Rodríguez of *AD*, since 1974 increased its debt by taking multiple loans. On 1 January 1976, oil was nationalised, and *Petróleos de Venezuela, S.A.* (*PDVSA*, Petroleum of Venezuela), Venezuela's national oil company, was established. In a short period of time, all oil-related activities carried out by foreign companies were taken over by subsidiaries of *PDVSA*. One year earlier, iron had been nationalised too.

In 1979, Pérez was succeeded by Luis Antonio Herrera Campins of *Copei*, who continued the policy of heavy borrowing. On 18 February 1983, however, the economic bubble exploded when the government devalued the Bolívar, the Venezuelan currency, making it lose 75 percent of its value. This day is known as the *Viernes Negro* (Black Friday), and since then the Venezuelan economy has been unable to return to its previous state of stability.

When Herrera Campins stepped down in 1984, he handed Jaime Ramón Lusinchi of *AD*, a country that was barely functional both institutionally and economically. The quality of life had collapsed, with 37.2 percent of the population living in poverty conditions by 1984. Two years later, this had risen to 59.1 percent, and by the end of the decade, it had reached an all-time high of 70 percent,[5] and corruption scandals led to the population rejecting the regime established in 1958.

On 2 February 1989, Carlos Andrés Pérez was sworn in as president for the second time, after a successful campaign promising to bring back the stability and prosperity that had characterised his first tenure. One of his first actions was to launch a program called *El Gran Viraje* (The Great Turn), which comprised a series of liberal economic measures recommended by the International Monetary Fund (IMF) that aimed to reduce the influence of the State in the economy and to produce an accelerated growth after a short period of sharp decline. In the meanwhile, the country would receive over 4.5 billion dollars from the IMF in different loans. This decision was the absolute opposite of what he had promised during his campaign, in which he accused the IMF and World Bank of being at the service of the economic elites.

From the first moment, the measures were unpopular among the population, especially the reduction of subsides for fuel and other oil derivates, as well as the increase in public transport fares. The increase of fuel prices had historically been a taboo for Venezuelan governments, as it has always led to civil unrest. 1989 was no exception to this, and less than one month into Pérez's presidency, starting on 27 February, the bloodiest riots the country has witnessed took place and resulted in a number of deaths that ranges from the official figure of 276 to the independent estimates that put the toll well above 3,000.

Even after the situation was controlled, in mid-March, the government remained highly unpopular, and a coup was seen as the most probable outcome of all the accumulated tension, which did not only exist among regular citizens, but also among the military. At this point, it is worth saying that, unlike other South American countries, including Argentina, Chile, and Uruguay, historically, in Venezuela, joining the military was not a popular option among the upper middle and high classes. The relatively few exceptions to this often join either the Air Force or the Navy, with the Army and the National Guard being more popular among the less-favoured groups. This was not true only for enlisted personnel, but also for the officer corps.

Such state of affairs shows that 27 February 1989 was an occasion on which those shooting and those being shot at had the same hardships at home. This is one of the main reasons that led to the conspiracies in the military that will be discussed later.

OPERATION POOR RICHARD

On 13 May 1958, during the visit of the US Vice President Richard M Nixon to Caracas, his motorcade was attacked by a mob while underway in downtown Caracas. Nowadays largely forgotten, at the time the affair was described as the 'most violent attack ever perpetrated on a high US official while on foreign soil.'

Nixon's visit took place only months after the coup against Marcos Pérez Jiménez: he arrived by aircraft and faced a crowd of demonstrators already at Maiquetía International Airport. Indeed, as Venezuelan troops and police essentially withdrew from the scene, the vice president and his party had to literally fight their way to cars protected by a thin line of US Secret Service agents. Nixon was to lay a wreath at the tomb of Simón Bolívar, however, as a large crowd had assembled there, this point in his itinerary was cancelled. Nevertheless, as his motorcade travelled through the Venezuelan capital, it was slowed down by heavy traffic and then surrounded by several hundred people, who began throwing stones at it. When the Venezuelan police refused to intervene, Nixon's bodyguards rushed to protect him: several were injured in the resulting melee, as was Nixon's wife, wounded by flying glass when the windows of the car in which she was riding were smashed.

Eventually, 12 minutes after the start of the incident, the motorcade – possibly supported by troops of the Venezuelan Army – managed to clear a path through the crowd and escape to the US Embassy, which by that time was surrounded by Venezuelan troops and the US Marine guards.

According to Venezuelan officials, the attack was organised by the *PCV*. However, this was never officially confirmed.

In reaction to this incident, Chief of Naval Operations of the US Navy, Admiral Arleigh Burke, initiated Operation Poor Richard. This included elements of the 2nd Marine Division and the 101st Airborne Division staging to bases in Puerto Rico and Guantánamo Bay, on Cuba, while the aircraft carrier USS *Tarawa* (CVS-40), along with eight destroyers and two amphibious assault ships was deployed towards Venezuela. By that point, the Venezuelans took care to significantly bolster the protection of Nixon's party.

Rioters attacking cars of Nixon's motorcade. (Albert Grandolini Collection)

An officer of the Venezuelan Military Police in next to Nixon's car. Although equipped with shatterproof glass, this was barely able to withstand the pummelling it received from the crowd. (US Government)

In reaction to the attack on Nixon's motorcade in Caracas, the Venezuelan Army significantly bolstered the protection of his party for the rest of the trip. (Albert Grandolini Collection)

1 THE VENEZUELAN ARMED FORCES

Venezuela has been characterised through its republican history as being a highly militarised country at all levels, from the high spheres of power in the government to the day-to-day life of the ordinary citizen. Proof of this is the fact that since 1810, the country has spent most of its existence under some sort of military rule, and that the military has, more often than not, been the main (and sometimes even the sole) support used by national leaders to stay in power.

The inception of the *Fuerzas Armadas Nacionales* (*FAN*, National Armed Forces) was very similar to that of other American countries, characterised by an irregular, guerrilla-like nature during its first years, which was ended by a period of unification and standardisation that eventually led to a process of professionalisation and growth.

One Country, Several Armies

The Military of Venezuela traces its roots back to the militia forces that fought the Spanish Empire through the Independence War from 1810 to 1823. The century that followed the declaration of independence was characterised by a lack of a national army, which, among other things, caused the country to lose almost 160,000km^2 of territory to the United Kingdom's colony of Guiana, which borders Venezuela to the east. Starting with the Independence War, the country suffered from chronic *caudillismo* until the first decade of the twentieth century.

For almost one hundred years, local strongmen imposed their will in different regions of the country, leaving Caracas, Venezuela's capital, as a symbolic prize for those who wanted to call themselves 'President of Venezuela'. Conflicts between the *caudillos* were common and widespread, especially after 1830, when Venezuela regained its independence from Colombia, which caused the country to be immersed in an almost uninterrupted state of civil war until approximately 1903.

The situation was prompted by a number of causes, one of which was the lack of a proper road network throughout the country. Most of the roads were rendered unusable by rainwater from May to December every year, which not only caused the government in Caracas to be unable to mobilise and supply troops deep in the country, but also made it impossible for representatives from most provinces to be able to attend government meetings in the capital. In this situation, different regions operated almost as if they were independent states.

In Venezuela, the figure of the *caudillo* differs considerably from one person to another and from one era to another. Thus, we find that the first generation of *caudillos* was composed on one side by independentist[1] landowners and slaveowners who fought against the Spaniards for economic reasons or just for being *afrancesados,*[2] and on the other side by Spaniards with a wide array of backgrounds who gathered soldiers both in the Iberian Peninsula and America and went to fight for the Spanish Crown. In the first group we find names like Simón Bolívar, José Antonio Páez Herrera or Manuel Carlos María Francisco Piar Gómez, while in the second the most emblematic were José Tomás Millán de Boves y de la Iglesia and Pablo Morillo y Morillo.

Through the Independence War, despite its militia-like nature, the *Ejército Libertador Venezolano* (Venezuelan Liberation Army, the semi-official name used by the independentist forces) operated with a chain of command with a clear leader, Simón Bolívar. This, however, does not mean that his leadership was uncontested; at various points during the war, Santiago Mariño Carige Fitzgerald, Carlos Valentín José de la Soledad Antonio del Sacramento de Soublette y Jerez de Aristeguieta and the aforementioned Manuel Piar defied Bolívar, the latter being executed for this reason in Angostura on 16 October 1817.

The second generation of *caudillos* started to arise in the mid-1820s, when Venezuelan officers started to conspire to separate Venezuela from the Gran Colombia, which had been formed in the Congress of Angostura on 17 December 1819, uniting Colombia, Ecuador, Panama and Venezuela in a single state. Their leader was José Antonio Páez, who had fought alongside Bolívar during the Independence War. He would eventually occupy the presidency of Venezuela three times, the first being in 1830, immediately after independence was achieved again. Bolívar would be banned from entering Venezuela, and eventually died on 17 December of that year in Santa Marta, Colombia, from tuberculosis.

After this, a new conflict emerged. It revolved between supporters of the *liberales* and the *conservadores* and was characterised by an intricate system of regional alliances between local strongmen and whoever occupied Caracas at the time. The climax of this situation was the Federal War from 1859 to 1863. The conflict, the biggest since the Independence War, left most of Venezuela in ruins and directly or indirectly caused the death of around 10 percent of the population, some 180,000 people. The conflict ended with the signing of the Treaty of Coche and a victory for the *liberales*, who, among other things, reduced the central government's army.

Although rebellions and minor clashes were common through the next four decades, none of them would match the Federal War in terms of human and material losses to the country. Only one rebellion, the *Revolución Liberal Restauradora* (Restorative Liberal Revolution), in 1899, had a deeper political impact for the country than the war of 1859. On 23 October, generals Cipriano Castro and Juan Vicente Gómez Chacón ousted General Ignacio Andrade Troconis, marking the beginning of the era of the *gochos.*[3]

Establishment of Regular Armed Forces

The formation of what today is called the *Fuerza Armada Nacional Bolivariana* (*FANB*, Bolivarian National Armed Force), the modern Armed Forces of Venezuela, was a slow, progressive process that developed through almost a decade. As soon as he became president, Castro realised that to be able to remain in power for a long time, he needed to get rid of the local *caudillos*. In consequence, he started to strengthen his own militia with modern equipment, training from foreign officers and increased manpower. At the same time, heavy investment in infrastructure, especially roads, made it easier for the government to project its power and influence in the countryside.

Two of the most important military events of the twentieth century in Venezuela took place at the same time. First, the *Revolución Libertadora* (Liberating Revolution), from 1901 to 1903. The last civil war of Venezuela involved the recently established *Ejército Venezolano* (Venezuelan Army) and militias loyal to José Manuel '*El Mocho*' Hernández, a *caudillo* who controlled parts of Guayana, Venezuela's gold-rich south-eastern region. Then, on

22 December 1902, a multi-national fleet with ships from Britain, Germany and Italy imposed a maritime blockade against Venezuela as the country was unable to pay reparations for damage to the properties of citizens from these countries (and others) suffered during the previous century's civil wars.

'*Venezolanos, la planta insolente del extranjero ha profanado el suelo de la patria...*' ('Venezuelans, the insolent foreign sole has desecrated the soil of our homeland...'), thus began the emotional speech delivered by Castro to announce to the country the presence of foreign forces that threatened the independence of Venezuela. He called all citizens to fight for Venezuela and evoked the victories in Carabobo and the Queseras del Medio,[4] during the Independence War.

The population dramatically supported Castro's call to arms, thousands volunteered to join the Army, among which were most of the country's prison inmates, who were liberated after the government declared a general amnesty. A truce was set up between *El Mocho* Hernández's forces and the government, and both armies started to prepare for an imminent invasion by the Europeans.

Episodes like the bombardments of Puerto Cabello and Fort San Carlos by the British and German navies, respectively, were the main events of the blockade. The crisis was eventually solved through diplomatic mediation from Argentina and the United States, which led to the withdrawal of the foreign fleet in February 1903 after Venezuela agreed, among other things, to give up its claims on the Dutch-controlled islands of Aruba, Bonaire and Curacao.

Juan Vicente Gómez, dictator of Venezuela from 1908 to 1935. Born into a prominent family of Andean landowners, he founded the country's first airline (Aeropostal - Alas de Venezuela) and the Venezuelan Air Force, was crucial in jump-starting the oil industry of the country and prompted sweeping reforms of the armed forces. (Library of Congress)

The civil war resumed almost as soon as the European fleet left and ended after the government took the last rebel stronghold in the Battle of Ciudad Bolívar, on 21 July 1903.

On 19 December 1908, Juan Vicente Gómez, then vice president and Castro's closest associate, staged a bloodless coup and took power. It was during his tenure, which would last until 1935, that the Venezuelan military became a formal, unified entity, leaving in the past the phenomenon of the local militias. Through Gómez's rule, infantry was the arm that developed the most, since the government's main fear was an internal rebellion. Infantry and, to a lesser degree, cavalry were considered the most effective forces to deploy in such a situation.

Venezuela's first standard issue weapon was the Mauser M71/84 rifle acquired after the demobilisation of the *Deutsches Heer* (Imperial German Army) after the end of First World War. The standardisation of the Army also included the issue of uniforms, something that until the 1910s was unheard of outside of the officer ranks. Furthermore, a new formal military culture had to be created from scratch, since the already existent militia-style perception of the soldier was not compatible with the new armed organisation. In this regard, the government promoted the image of the armed forces as an institution of armed citizens, who were useful and worthy members of society tasked with the protection of Venezuela's independence and territorial integrity.

In 1910, the various military formation centres already existing in the country were united as the *Escuela Militar de Venezuela* (Military School of Venezuela). However, no institution for higher military studies was created until decades later. Thus, the training and education of Venezuelan generals was carried out in foreign military academies, mainly in Colombia and Peru.

Another important development during Gómez's tenure was the arrival of aviation in the country, both of civilian and military nature. On 29 September 1912, the first flight in Venezuela took off. Next year, the government set up a commission to create an aerial unit for the Army. The beginning of the First World War would delay the procurement of airplanes as all available aircraft manufacturers were working for the belligerent countries. Thus, it would not be until 1920 that a mission of French instructors and technicians landed in Caracas with a Caudron G.3 which would become Venezuela's first military aircraft. The same year, Gómez ordered the establishment of the *Escuela de Aviación Militar* (*EAM*, School of Military Aviation), in Maracay.

Through Gómez's era, the *FAN* remained heavily politicised, and although it was no longer an irregular force, *El Benemérito* retained the personalism that characterises *caudillismo*. This would come to an end after his passing on 17 December 1935, when General Eleazar López Contreras started to reform the political apparatus. On 4 August 1937, the *Guardia Nacional de Venezuela* (Venezuelan National Guard), the national gendarmerie, was established.

In 1938, two second-hand Azio-class gunboat-converted minelayers were bought from Italy, *Milazzo* and *Dardanelli* were renamed *General Urdaneta* and *General Soublette*, respectively. The Italian-built ships were two of the only three gunboats the *Armada Venezolana* (Venezuelan Navy) had that were not originally designed for civilian service. The third was *Miranda*, a Ponce de León-class gunboat delivered to the Spanish Navy in October 1895 under the name of *Diego de Velázquez*. It was captured in Cuba during the Hispano-American War and later sold to Venezuela.

Three additional gunboats, *José Félix Ribas*, *General Salom* and *Aragua* were tugboats fitted with naval guns. Other minor ships included *El Leandro*, the presidential yacht; *Naricual*, a training

A column of five Venezuelan-built Tortuga reconnaissance cars. Essentially, they consisted of a locally-designed armoured hull on the chassis of the 1934 Ford 6x4 truck. They were the first armoured vehicles manufactured locally. (Albert Grandolini Collection)

ship property of the Naval Academy; and *Mariscal Sucre*, an Isla de Luzón-class gunboat originally delivered to the Spanish Navy in 1897 with the name *Isla de Cuba*. It was sunk the following year in Cavite, in the Philippines, salvaged by the Americans in 1899 and sold to Venezuela in 1912. By 1939 it was not seaworthy and only used as a static training centre.

In 1939 the Venezuelan Army was composed of approximately 6,000 men, organised into 10 brigades, one cavalry regiment and one artillery regiment. The standard issue weapon for infantry was the FN Modéle 1924/30. Less standardised was the artillery regiment, which used a mix of German, French and Italian cannons and howitzers of different calibres, which often caused logistical and supply problems. Additionally, the armoured corps operated a small fleet of two Fiat-Ansaldo CV.33s.

On the other hand, the air arm, which at the time was a regiment of the Army called *Regimiento Militar de Aviación N°1*, was equipped with three Dewoitine D.500s and nine Fiat CR.32 fighters, six Fleet Model 10s, three North American NA-16s and three Morane-Saulnier MS.147 trainers. Additionally, 12 Breguet Bre.19s, three Curtiss-Wright C.14R Ospreys, a single Fiat BR.20 and three bomber-converted Latécoère 28s were the Venezuelan Army's ground attack platforms.

The Army's combat capability, however, remained limited as its main mission of foiling internal dissent and uprisings rather than fighting an organised force prevailed for years after Gómez's death.

Venezuela, the Second World War and the Early Cold War: Keeping up with the Times

López Contreras was succeeded by General Isaías Medina Angarita in 1941. The new president had been considered ideologically close to the Italian Fascism before taking office, however after he was sworn in, he maintained López Contreras' policy of favouring the Allies and claiming to be neutral at the same time. Shortly into his tenure, the supply of Venezuelan oil to Germany was cut after the United States pressured the Venezuelan government to do so. This caused the *Kriegsmarine* to launch Operation *Neuland*,[5] which sought to disrupt the oil supply to the United States and the United Kingdom.

German U-Boats sank 45 cargo ships between February 1942 and July 1944, among which were the Venezuelan-crewed *Pedernales*, *San Nicolás*, *Tía Juana*, *San Rafael* and *Monagas*. The latter, sunk by *U-502*, being the only one flying a Venezuelan flag. In response, the United States sent a group of advisors to Venezuela to help the country improve its capability to patrol its coast.

In 1941, Caracas and Washington signed a Lend-Lease agreement which aimed at helping Venezuela prepare to defend itself in case the Axis attacked the country. One of the first shipments of military hardware for Venezuela consisted of 18 M3A1 Stuart light tanks. A variety of equipment for the Army followed, from Thompson SMGs to M8 Greyhound armoured vehicles.

The air arm, at the time still part of the Army, also received a considerable amount of equipment. Nine Curtiss-Wright SNC-1 trainers were the first aircraft delivered under Lend-Lease. In the next years, and until the end of the war, a further three NA-16s, three T-6 Texans, two Stearman A76s and 20 Fairchild PT-19s were handed to the Venezuelan military.

Although the government considered the Navy to be the branch that needed new equipment the fastest, it was not until 1944 that the United States transferred four 83-foot patrol boats fitted with anti-submarine equipment. The new ships were named *Antonio Díaz*, *Brión*, *Briceño Méndez* and *Arismendi*. This was the only significant addition to the Venezuelan fleet under Lend-Lease, although other minor gunboats were delivered, mainly armed tug ships.

After the war ended, Medina Angarita, through an executive decree, established the *Infantería de Marina* (Marine Infantry) by merging two ship-protection companies into the *1er Batallón de Infantería de Marina Simón Bolívar*, the precursor of the current marine corps of Venezuela. Before that, the country lacked a specialised naval landing unit.

Shortly after the Axis surrendered, on 18 October 1945 Medina Angarita was ousted by a group of young military officers that had been conspiring with *Acción Democrática* since 1943. Among the reasons cited for their involvement in the uprising were the low salaries they were paid and the prevalence of cronyism within the *FAN*. The fall of Medina Angarita marked the end of an era which

A pair of M3A1 Stuart light tanks, donated by the USA in 1942. (Albert Grandolini Collection)

Another armoured vehicle supplied by the USA during the Second World War was the M3 White scout car, here armed with a Browning 12.7mm heavy machine gun. (Albert Grandolini Collection)

In 1947, Venezuela received the first three Douglas C-47 Skytrain transports, and by the late 1950s as many as 20 had served with the FAV. Although some six or seven were written off over the years, a few were still operational as of the 1980s. (Albert Grandolini Collection)

saw the military, especially the Army, control almost all aspects of the country's political life.

The new government, the *Junta Revolucionaria de Gobierno*, continued the arms purchases that started with the previous administration. Although the US Department of State did not trust *AD* immediately after the coup, they considered that continued cooperation with the new Venezuelan government would strengthen the relations between both countries and bring closer the already US-friendly members of the *junta*.

US ambassador to Venezuela, Francis Patrick Corrigan, expressed in a meeting with a representative of the Department of State his concern about what he described as 'the compulsive requests of modern military hardware, and specially of modern aircraft, by the Venezuelan Ministry of Defence led by Carlos Delgado Chalbaud.' He was especially concerned about the request for 14 Republic P-47 Thunderbolts, whose performance and firepower he considered to be well above the Venezuelans' needs. Corrigan suggested that the planes be delivered only after a democratic government was elected in a free and fair election. One of the reasons that led to the request for the Thunderbolts was that Venezuela had not had a true fighter aircraft in service since 1942, when the CR.32s were phased out.

Eventually, in 1947, the US government decided to deliver six Thunderbolts and three Douglas C-47 Dakotas to the Venezuelan Air Force, which had become an independent branch of the *FAN* the previous year as the *Fuerza Aérea Venezolana* (*FAV*, Venezuelan Air Force). The six new fighters were assigned to the *Escuadrón de Caza 10* of the *Grupo Mixto de Caza y Reconocimiento 9*, based in the Generalísimo Francisco de Miranda Airbase, in Caracas. The same year, the first deliveries of an order for 14 North American B-25J Mitchells took place, being assigned to the *Escuadrón de Bombardeo 3* and *Escuadrón de Bombardeo 7*, based in Maracay.

Further purchases of T-6 Texans elevated the number of operational aircraft to 16. A remarkable acquisition at the time was a batch of four Sikorsky S-51s for the Air Force, one of which was intended for presidential use. Those were the first helicopters operated by any of the branches of the *FAN*. It is also worth mention that the first presidential airplane of Venezuela was also acquired in this period, a Douglas C-54 Skymaster.

On 24 November 1948 another coup took place, putting an end to the short presidency of Rómulo Gallegos and bringing the military back into power. The *Junta Militar de Gobierno*, led by Carlos Delgado Chalbaud, had been established.

The new government reverted some of the reforms introduced by Medina Angarita, Betancourt – head of the *Junta Revolucionaria* – and Gallegos. Most of the changes were aimed at bringing the State and the *FAN* closer. Thus, the government and many of its agencies were led mostly by indoctrinated military officers. The militarisation of the governmental apparatus increased after Delgado Chalbaud's assassination in 1950, with the accession to power of General Pérez Jiménez.

The reforms also affected the military, which saw its structure and doctrine changed. Despite the incorporation of new equipment in the previous years, the Venezuelan armed forces' structure was not aimed at fighting an external enemy, but rather internal dissent. Its inability to defend the country's interests were evidenced in 1941, when López Contreras was forced to sign a border demarcation agreement with Colombia, in which Venezuela gave up its claim on approximately 200,000 km^2 of Colombian-occupied territory.

The *Junta Militar* aimed at recovering all the territory Venezuela had lost since its independence, arguing that the legitimate boundaries of the country were those of the Captaincy General of Venezuela at the time of its establishment in 1777. Thus, the new

In the aftermath of the 1948 coup d'état that ousted Rómulo Gallegos, multiple caches of weapons were hidden by his supporters in order to start an insurgency against the new military government. However, these were quickly discovered and confiscated by the authorities. Pictured is one found in a school in the eastern city of Cumaná, in the state of Sucre. (Albert Grandolini Collection)

In 1952, Venezuela placed its first order for English Electric Canberra medium bombers. By 1958, the *FAV* acquired 16 B.Mk 2s, B(I).Mk 8s, and T.Mk 4s. Additional acquisitions for B(I).Mk 88s, T.Mk 84s, and B(I)I.Mk 82s in the mid-1960s eventually brought the total number of Canberras operated by the Venezuelan Air Force to nearly 40. (Albert Grandolini Collection)

One of the T-6s assigned to the *Grupo Escuela Aviacion Militar* (Military Aviation School), seen shortly before landing. Starting in 1942, the *FAV* acquired a total of four AT-6Bs, 14 AT-6Cs, eight AT-6Ds, and 21 T-6Cs, 20 T-6Ds, and T-30Gs. They remained in service until 1992. (Albert Grandolini Collection)

A scene from a military parade held on 5 July 1954, when multiple M8 Greyhound armoured cars passed in front of the presidential tribune during the annual military parade held on Independence Day. Above them is a Sikorsky S-51. (Albert Grandolini Collection)

potential enemies the *FAN* would face were the armies of Brazil, Colombia and the United Kingdom. The first campaign would be against the British colony of Guiana and was scheduled to take place between 1958 and 1963.

It was considered impractical to modernise or even keep operating any of the military equipment that had been acquired by 1948 in the medium term. In consequence, investment in defence increased on a par with oil revenues, which prompted the Venezuelan government to buy state-of-the-art hardware for all branches of the *FAN*. One of the first purchases was a batch of 8,000 FN Modéle 1949/SAFN rifles, which became the standard issue weapon of the Army.

Although there was no preferred country to buy equipment from, due to the nature of the new Venezuelan regime, the Soviet Union was never approached when the main Western powers refused to deliver weapons to Venezuela. A staunch anti-communist, Pérez Jiménez considered that by showing loyalty to the West, he would eventually be given what he asked for.

Venezuela had showed interest in the de Havilland Vampire since it was introduced in the Royal Air Force in 1946. However, as consequence of the United Kingdom's reluctance to provide them in 1948, one of the first acquisitions of the new regime were 22 additional Thunderbolt Ds that were delivered in July 1949. The same month, the British finally agreed to provide 24 Vampires in its FB.Mk.52 version, with the first four aircraft being delivered in December. These were the first jet aircraft operated by the Venezuelan military. Between 1952 and 1958, six T.Mk.55 trainers were acquired.

In October 1952, after a goodwill visit by four Royal Air Force English Electric Canberras which created a good impression upon the Venezuelan officers, the *FAV* placed an order for six English Electric Canberra B.Mk.2s which were delivered between March and July 1953. One of the aircraft was lost in an accident on 8 November 1954. Another 10 Canberras were ordered in late-1956, eight B.(I).Mk.8s and two T.Mk.4s trainers. These were assigned to *Escuadrón de Bombardeo 40* at first, with the entire fleet of this type later being transferred to the newly formed *Escuadrón de Bombardeo 39* in 1957.

The B-25 fleet was also increased, with 10 second-hand J versions bought from the US Air Force in 1952 and a further nine in 1953 from the Royal Canadian Air Force. At least one H version was delivered in 1955, which was followed by the last five in 1957. *Escuadrón de Bombardeo 3* and *7*, which operated the first Mitchells, were merged in 1952, forming *Escuadrón de Bombardeo 40*.

In mid-1954, the *FAV* placed an order for 22 de Haviland Venom FB.Mk.54s, the first being delivered in February 1955. These saw service in a newly established unit, *Escuadrón de Caza 34*. By the end of the year, the first three of an order of 22 ex-USAF North American F-86F Sabres were delivered, the first supersonic aircraft to be used by the *FAV*. These new planes had entirely replaced the Thunderbolts by late-1956. Other purchases for the Air Force

Four *FAV* pilots proudly posing in front of a row of North American F-86F Sabres acquired in 1956. The type remained in service into the 1970s, and – starting in 1967 – was reinforced by acquisitions of F-86Ks. (Albert Grandolini Collection)

included five Sikorsky H-19 Chickasaws, 18 Fairchild C-123 Providers, and additional T-6 Texan trainer aircraft.

The Navy was also included in the modernisation efforts, commissioning three Nueva Esparta-class destroyers: ARV *Aragua*,[6] ARV *Nueva Esparta*, and ARV *Zulia*, built by Vickers-Armstrong in England, between 1953 and 1956. Six Italian-built Almirante Clemente-class light destroyers were also delivered and commissioned in 1956 and 1957: ARV *Almirante Brión*, ARV *Almirante Clemente*, ARV *Almirante José García*, ARV *General José de Austria*, ARV *General José Trinidad Morán* and ARV *General Juan José Flores*.

However, the Army was the branch that underwent the deepest reforms, both at the administrative and operational levels. For the campaign in Guiana, the *Junta* considered that it needed an army of at least 125,000 men, 30,000 of them specially trained to fight in the jungle. In 1955, the FN FAL started to replace the M1 Garand and the FN Modéle 1949/SAFN as standard issue rifle in the Venezuelan Army.

New armoured units were also created. By 1948, the only tanks Venezuela had were 18 Stuarts delivered under Lend-Lease in the 1940s and approximately 10 Venezuelan-built *Tortuga* reconnaissance vehicles. In 1953, a batch of 40 M18A1 Hellcat tank destroyers were delivered to the Venezuelan Army. Two years later, in 1955, a similar number of AMX-13M51s were acquired from France. The Hellcats were assigned to the *Batallón Blindado José Francisco Bermúdez*, in Caracas, while the AMX-13s were sent to the *Batallón Blindado Bravos de Apure*, in San Juan de los Morros.

2 UPRISINGS AND COUPS

Pérez Jiménez did not have to face a strong and organised armed opposition. While political assassinations were not a rarity, the authors, often members of *Acción Democrática* and the *Partido Comunista de Venezuela*, were rapidly caught by the *DSN*. However, despite the continuous indoctrination effort within the *FAN*, dissent existed among the ranks. Due to the effectiveness of the intelligence apparatus, Pérez Jiménez only had to face three major military uprisings, two of which he was able to suppress.

The first uprising came on 28 September 1952, when Captain Wilfrido Omaña and Lieutenant Héctor Navarro Torres led an uprising in the Mariscal Sucre Airbase in Maracay. They managed to have their forces control the city for four hours, but the situation was rapidly brought under control by the *DSN*. Omaña would escape that day, joining the underground forces that conspired against the government, but would be killed eventually on 24 February 1954 by agents of the *DSN* during a shootout in Caracas.

After General Pérez Jiménez fled the country shortly after midnight on 23 January 1958, thousands of *AD*, *Copei*, *URD* and *PCV* supporters flooded the streets as they celebrated. There were instances of violence against identified members of the *Seguridad Nacional*, specially at the agency's headquarters, whose car park is here depicted after being burned down by protesters. (Albert Grandolini Collection)

In the aftermath of the January 1958 coup d'état, there were multiple attempts both from the military and from political entities to overthrow the government and attain political power. Pictured here is a loyalist column of M18 Hellcat tank destroyers heading to combat rebels during the uprising that took place on 7 September that year. (Albert Grandolini Collection)

The second rebellion took place on 1 January 1958. On 15 December 1957, a plebiscite was held. Electors could vote 'yes' or 'no' depending on whether they wanted Pérez Jiménez to lead the country for another five years. The results, which were rapidly considered fraudulent, gave a wide victory to 'yes'. Immediately after, a group of officers led by Colonel Hugo Enrique Trejo started to plan an operation to oust the government. The date set was New Year's Day. The uprising began with a pair of Vampires strafing Miraflores Palace, which is the seat of the Presidency. Military support for the rebellion was less than initially expected, and after multiple troop movements through the Valencia-Maracay-Caracas axis through the day, the situation was controlled by the government by midnight.

The next three weeks were at the time described as Venezuela's most tense. The military high command was replaced twice, repression increased to levels never seen before, rioting and strikes were an everyday thing, and hospitals could not handle the amount of injured people they received from street protests. Due to a significant cabinet restructuring on 10 January, the last 12 days of Pérez Jiménez's rule were characterised by the lack of a clear and strong leadership in governmental bodies. The security apparatus also became increasingly paranoid, imprisoning some members from Pérez Jiménez's inner circle who were suspected to be conspirators, as well as officers from the *FAN* for the same reason.

The military government had never been in such a vulnerable position, and the opposition was aware of that. The Navy was approached, and after a meeting, Rear Admiral Wolfgang Larrazábal Ugüeto was chosen to preside over the transitional *junta* that would be established after Pérez Jiménez was dismissed.

22 January seemed like any other day, with protests, rumours and clashes between the opposition and police forces in the streets. However, as night arrived, the destroyers ARV *Aragua* and ARV *Zulia* set sail as their base in Puerto Cabello rebelled against the government. In a short time, most military units in the areas surrounding Caracas adhered to the uprising, including the *Escuela*

Militar, which was in Caracas itself. This was the breaking point. After being told that the cadets had also revolted, Pérez Jiménez ordered his circle to prepare to leave at around 21:30 as he considered that killing young cadets was a disgraceful thing to do. He left Miraflores Palace at 01:15 of the 23rd, arriving at the Generalísimo Francisco de Miranda Airbase before 02:00. Approximately at 03:00, *La Vaca Sagrada* (The Sacred Cow), the popular name given to the C-54 Skymaster that served as presidential aircraft, took off bound for Ciudad Trujillo, now Santo Domingo, in the Dominican Republic. Besides his family, other members of the government, including Luis Llovera Páez, were aboard the plane. The fact that it was not intercepted or shot down has raised dispute over whether he was allowed to leave by the putschists or simply managed to escape.

A Troubled Multiparty Experiment

Two short, transitional administrations were replaced by an elected government led by Rómulo Betancourt in 1959. Despite high rates of approval from the population, the nascent Venezuelan multiparty system was weak through its first years. It was threatened mainly by two groups: radical leftists who were unhappy with their exclusion from the arrangement that would determine the dynamic of the Venezuelan political life for the next four decades, and by members from the *FAN* who did not agree with the path the country was being taken to. The latter group can be divided in two: nationalists and leftists.

After being marginalised from national-level politics, the leadership of the *PCV* decided to start a 'people's war' during the party's Third Congress, in 1960. The same year, another party that would join the armed struggle was founded, it was known as the *Movimiento de Izquierda Revolucionaria* (*MIR*, Revolutionary Left Movement). In 1961, in the northern state of Lara, the first guerrilla group associated with the *PCV* was established, its name was *Frente Libertador Simón Bolívar* (Simón Bolívar Liberation Front). Prior to that, small actions of partisan nature had been carried out by the *Frente Unido de Liberación* (*FUL*, United Liberation Front), a loose umbrella organisation of about 60 small armed groups based mainly in northern Venezuela.

Even before the communists considered forming a guerrilla movement to fight against the government, the nationalist sector of the *FAN* staged its first attempt to seize power in the early hours of 7 September 1958. A group of officers led by lieutenant colonels Juan de Dios Moncada Vidal and José Eli Mendoza Méndez, as well as Major Manuel Asuaje Ortega, mutinied in Caracas. The plan was to take the Police Academy in El Junquito, 10 kilometres west of the city, while the barracks of the Military Police situated close to Miraflores Palace revolted simultaneously. Major Luis Alberto Vivas Ramírez oversaw the operation in El Junquito, from where he took his men to Caracas and captured a radio station: *Radio Rumbos*. Moncada Vidal, along with captains Carlos Quintero Florido, José de Jesús Chacón and Carlos González Windevoxhel oversaw the operations in Caracas, which included the occupation of the Ministry of Defence and Miraflores Palace. Overall, the rebellion was intended to be a *pronunciamiento*, as its leaders expected other military units from the provinces to join them as soon as the news of the uprising became known.

Although in the early hours of the uprising the putschists had managed to capture most of their objectives, lack of support from other military units rapidly doomed the operation. Furthermore, pro-government forces had taken over the TV channel *Televisa* and the station of *Radio Caracas*, from where the population was called to the streets to reject the coup. Combat ensued between rebel and loyalist forces in the main political centres of the country, ultimately causing 20 deaths and over 150 injured. By mid-afternoon, some rebel leaders started to surrender, while others went to seek refuge in the embassy of Mexico, among whom were Moncada Vidal and Vivas Ramírez.

Putschist Attempts of 1961 and 1962

Less than two years later, in April 1960, and one year and two months into Betancourt's tenure, another right-wing takeover plan was set in motion. This time, retired Colonel Jesús María Castro León crossed into Venezuela with a group of sympathisers he had amassed in the Colombian border town of Cúcuta, took the city of San Cristóbal and held it for seven hours before his men were forced to fall back to Colombia after being unable to stop the advance from the loyalists.

Castro León, a nationalist, was supported in Venezuela by former agents of the *DSN* who had managed to escape the purges of 1958. They provided him with intelligence about the current status of the *FAN* and contacted some officers that might have joined the rebels once combat started. It is unclear whether they had any success in finding support in other units, but if they initially did, the compromised officers failed to react when combat broke out.

It has been reported that nationalists and *perezjimenistas*[1] received political and material support from Rafael Leonidas Trujillo, longtime ruler of the Dominican Republic and opponent to any process of democratisation in Latin America, as well as a close friend of Pérez Jiménez. In fact, less than two months after Castro León's failure, during the celebrations of the 139th anniversary of the victory in the Battle of Carabobo, an attempt to assassinate Betancourt with a car bomb failed. Trujillo was accused of being the mastermind behind the attack, which brought both countries to the verge of war. The conflict was ultimately prevented after members of the Organization of American States unanimously decided to punish the Dominican regime through sanctions.

Even though Castro León was not a *perezjimenista* himself, having been a key participant in the rebellion against Pérez Jiménez on 1 January 1958, his differences with the former ruler were merely personal, sharing most of their views on what the path the country goes through should be.

Other members from the military that were not linked to Pérez Jiménez, but still considered themselves as nationalists, also tried to overthrow the government. On 26 June 1961 in the coastal city of Barcelona, the capital of the state of Anzoátegui, a brief uprising occurred, known as *El Barcelonazo*.

Two retired officers, majors Luis Alberto Vivas Ramírez, mentioned previously, and Rubén Massó, and one active, Captain Tesalio Murillo took control of the *Pedro María Freites* garrison after kidnapping various officials from the regional government, including the governor himself. One of the conspirators, Elonis López Curra, openly described the uprising as 'rightist … having the goal of establishing a military government in Venezuela.' Murillo himself said that the goals '…were the same of all [putschist] movements, overthrowing the government and attaining political power.'[2]

The leaders expected that other units would join their cause once the news of the uprising spread through Venezuela. It did not happen, and the loyalist counterattack started at 07:00, three hours after the rebels captured the garrison. By 10:00, the rebellion had been thwarted. There were 37 casualties between the two sides, including 18 dead.

Three Coups of 1962

1962 saw three attempts to overthrow the government during its first six months. All of them were linked to armed communist organisations. It is worth mentioning that at the time of their inception, these groups did not intend to wage a long war of attrition like their counterparts in Colombia and Guatemala, as the leadership considered a single putsch in conjunction with the military as the best way to take over the country.

With this scenario in mind, the first attempted rebellion of this nature took place on 28 February 1962, in the coastal city of La Guaira. The plan was that Corvette Captain Victor Hugo Morales Monasterios, the officer in command of the *1er Batallón de Infantería de Marina Simón Bolívar*, was to take control of the surroundings of the garrison of his unit and wait for some 300 members of the militant wing of the *MIR* in the city, which was led by Teodoro Petkoff Malek, to arrive at the place. The insurgents would be given weapons and uniforms while other units, among which were the members of the 99th Detachment of the National Guard, in Maiquetía, and the 8th Mechanised Infantry Regiment, in Caracas, revolted.

The 8th Regiment was tasked with marching towards Miraflores Palace, the seat of the presidency. Meanwhile, the troops from La Guaira and Puerto Cabello would be on their way to act as reinforcements for the assault. 28 February was picked because a gathering had been convoked that day to protest an increase in public transportation fares.

Loyalist troops during the fighting in Puerto Cabello, in early June 1962. (Albert Grandolini Collection)

A mortar team of loyalist troops outside Puerto Cabello. The town was partially under rebel control after local units of the *Infantería de Marina* revolted against the government. (Albert Grandolini Collection)

That day, however, when Petkoff and his men arrived at the gates of the garrison, he was met by a hesitant Morales Monasterios, who argued that the circumstances were not ideal at that moment and that the rebellion should be postponed, asking him to retire his people. When Petkoff refused to do so, the officer called the police, which promptly arrested more than 200 of the *MIR* militants.

Petkoff and other leaders managed to escape, and although Morales Monasterios' insurrectional tendencies were not revealed until later, he was considered suspicious by the high command and transferred to a non-vital job in the naval base of Puerto Cabello. Months later, he would actively participate in another failed uprising, for which he faced a trial. During the process against him, his involvement in La Guaira surfaced, being ultimately sentenced to 30 years of imprisonment.

A new rebellion began at 02:00 on 2 May in the northeastern city of Carúpano, on the Caribbean coast, when the commander of the *3er Batallón de Infantería de Marina Antonio José de Sucre*, Corvette Captain Jesús Teodoro Molina Villegas, made a *pronunciamiento* against the Betancourt government. Upon learning about the new uprising, the 33rd Detachment of the National Guard, under command of Major Pedro Rigoberto Vargas Castejón and Captain Omar Echeverría Sierra, joined the movement. Militants of the *PCV* and *MIR*, some of whom were students from the local school who had been on strike for a few days when the rebellion started, also joined it.

The rebels quickly took control of Carúpano, using a captured Fokker F-27 airliner that belonged to Avensa, one of the country's largest airlines at the time, to conduct observation flights of the surroundings of the city. Having captured the local radio station, Molina Villegas read what he called the Manifesto of the Carúpano Garrison. The neighbouring villages of Río Caribe, Macarapana and San José de Aerocuar also fell under control of the rebels. In the manifesto, the group referred to itself as the *Movimiento de Recuperación* Nacional (Movement of National Recovery).

After sunrise, loyalists started to attack rebel positions from the air using Canberras, B-25s and F-86s. Approximately 1,500 marines from the *Simón Bolívar* and *Rafael Urdaneta* battalions disembarked on the city's beaches, quickly gaining a beachhead that was used to bring in heavy equipment. At the same time, the Army surrounded the area under rebel control, isolating it from the rest of the country, leaving them with no escape routes, and pounding their positions with heavy artillery.

Unable to improve their situation or to convince other units to join them, the rebels surrendered. In the end, there had been around 400 of them. The uprising claimed 15 lives, 14 military and one civilian.

Before the rebels laid down their arms, President Betancourt accused the *PCV* and *MIR* of being the main organisations behind the uprising, issuing Decree 752, *de facto* rendering illegal both parties and calling for the arrest of the leadership.

The last uprising was also the bloodiest one. Past midnight, on 2 June, only 29 days after the events in Carúpano, captains Pedro Medina Silva and Manuel Ponte Rodríguez, called for a rebellion against the Betancourt administration. They were officers of the *2do Batallón de Infantería de Marina Rafael Urdaneta*, that less than a month before had disembarked to foil another rebellion. This time, the city of choice was Puerto Cabello, also on the Caribbean coast. The rebels set up their headquarters in the Solano Fortress, a fortification built by the Spanish colonial authorities in the sixteenth century.

Rebels quickly took control of part of the city and its naval base. In the process, they liberated around 80 prisoners belonging to the *PCV* and *MIR* guerrillas that were caged in a local police station and gave them weapons. Once again, the local radio station was used to read a manifesto signed by the same group from Carúpano, the *Movimiento de Recuperación Nacional*.

Puerto Cabello hosts one of Venezuela's main naval bases. When the uprising took place, four destroyers (one of which, the ARV *Zulia*, was not seaworthy due to ongoing repairs), one LSM and several tugs were docked in the complex.

As in the previous events, the commanders of the uprising hoped that other units would join them when news about the uprising reached them. Members of the *PCV* had talked beforehand with officers from other units, including those of the 55th Detachment of the National Guard, based in Puerto Cabello, and expected their cooperation. However, this unit was the first one to oppose the rebels as they advanced through the city. Later, other units whose commanders had been approached by the political actors of the uprising and had expressed their support for it took part in the loyalist effort to retake the city.

Shortly after the fighting erupted, the three seaworthy destroyers docked in the base sailed and began shelling rebel positions. Hours later, the rebels managed to capture the ARV *Zulia* with the help of some sailors that sympathised with their cause. However, they were unable to operate the turrets of the ship and return fire against the loyalists.

Unlike the previous uprisings, the *Porteñazo* was characterised by long, intense and bloody combats. Fighting ensued house to house, street to street, under periodic bursts of artillery and bombs from the same planes that helped control the situation in Carúpano.

Approximately at 11:00 the most emblematic moment of the uprising took place: Father Luis María Padilla, chaplain of the city's naval base, was photographed by Héctor Rondón Lovera, a graphic journalist working for *La República*, holding Andrés de Jesús Garcés, a soldier that had been hit by machine gun fire moments before and who died shortly after. The picture, named *La Ayuda del cura* (The Father's Assistance) won that year's Pulitzer Prize and remains an icon whenever the task of clergymen in the armed forces is addressed.

Weather was poor, but this did not stop the bombing raids. On the ground, rebels started to fall back as soon as the loyalist reinforcements arrived, often leaving snipers behind enemy lines, which slowed the advances and dramatically increased casualties on the loyalist side.

As night arrived, the intensity of combat diminished, resulting in only a few small skirmishes during the dark. However, as soon as daylight arrived, the weather improved, and although it was nowhere close to clear, the raids by the Canberras were more frequent and precise.

The rebels managed to resist until shortly before 20:00, when just a few blocks of the city remained under their control, most of which were not connected to each other. White flags started to be hoisted, and by midnight all rebels had laid down their arms.

The number of casualties remains a matter of dispute today. While the first official account after the end of hostilities was a total of 135 deaths, other sources claim over 250 and even 400 for just the rebels.

After the thwarting of the *Porteñazo*, potential putschists within the *FAN* were demoralised by the quick succession of failures their comrades had suffered in just two years. Many officers suspected of being either communists, *perezjimenistas* or apathetic to the regime were placed under close surveillance from the *Dirección General de Policía* (*DIGEPOL*), the successor of the *DSN*.

An AMX-13 light tank supported by infantry on the streets of Puerto Cabello. (Albert Grandolini Collection)

Venezuelan Marines surrendering en masse at the end of the uprising in Puerto Cabello. (Albert Grandolini Collection)

In this situation, the guerrillas realised that they had to change their tactics, now intending to wage a long war of attrition against the government.

FALN Insurgency

On 1 January 1963, an umbrella organisation, the *Fuerzas Armadas de Liberación Nacional* (*FALN*, Armed Forces of National Liberation) was created by the now-illegal *PCV* and *MIR*. It grouped together all the leftist guerrilla organisations that were active at the time.[3] It is estimated that at the time of the establishment of the *FALN*, there were between 200 and 1,000 guerrilla fighters in the country, both in the jungle and in the cities. Political violence was condemned by some members of the political organisations that were linked to *FALN*, but according to Douglas Ignacio Bravo Mora,[4] it was a small group and the guerrilla action was supported by the vast majority of the political sphere of the left.

Unlike in neighbouring Colombia, in Venezuela the guerrillas failed to gain a base of support among the urban population for several reasons, among which was their well-known association with Cuba, whose increasingly authoritarian regime was a cause of concern for Venezuelans. Consequently, these groups were unable to effectively hold and control territory, with their activities being limited to hiding in the jungle and ambushing military patrols, as well as some actions of partisan-like nature such as minor attacks on the US Embassy in Caracas and the kidnapping of several American military advisors to Venezuela, like Colonel James Chenault and Lieutenant Colonel Michael Smolem,[5] and also of celebrities, like Alfredo di Stefano, a famous football player for Real Madrid.

Although the *FALN* did not represent a serious threat to the government, their activities attracted a considerable amount of media attention because at the time Venezuela was seen from outside as one of the most prosperous and stable countries in the region due to high oil prices that fuelled investment in infrastructure and welfare programs. However, poverty remained endemic and widespread.

One of the guerrillas' most famous operations, codenamed *Operación Olga Luzardo*, took place on 29 September 1963, when an assault on the Caracas-El Encanto train left five members of the National Guard dead and several passengers injured, while the attackers did not suffer any casualties. The media coverage of the event was decisive in the decline of the already small popular support for the armed movement, and the government used this as an excuse to crack down on supporters and suspected members of the *FALN* throughout the country.

Although troubles continued through the first year of Raúl Leoni's presidency, by 1965 the guerrillas were starting to wane due to the political defeat that the successful election of December 1963 represented for them. Furthermore, through 1964 and 1965, a series of offensives by government forces caused significant loses to most insurgent groups operating in the countryside, while the *Unidades Tácticas de Combate* (*UTC*, Tactical Combat Units), the communists' urban cells, were unable to react in the cities. The continuous defeats and the loss of popular support produced a sort of schism in the Venezuelan left, with members of the political sector openly condemning the armed struggle, and the armed sector accusing the former of cooperating with the government. Among the figures that laid down their weapons in 1965 were Domingo Alberto Rangel, secretary general of *MIR*; Pompeyo Ezequiel Márquez Millán, Guillermo García Ponce and Teodoro Petkoff, who had close links with the central committee of the *PCV*. In a common manifesto, they all called for the 'opening of a new tactical period, in which, instead of combining all forms of struggle, the actions of the guerrillas and *UTC* will be suspended, while political initiatives will be placed in the foreground.'[6]

With *FALN* guerrillas avoiding direct clashes with pursuing Army units, bigger firefights remained rare even during the manhunt for surviving insurgents that went on into the late 1960s. This group of Army troops are seen armed with FN FAL assault rifles. (Albert Grandolini Collection)

Despite the heavy blows, *FALN* continued to operate and receive support from abroad. One of the most important events occurred on 2 May 1967, when a group of 12 Cuban-trained guerrillas, eight Venezuelans and four Cubans, set sail for Venezuela from Santiago de Cuba. Their goal was to act as reinforcements for a cell of the *MIR* – now part of the *FALN* – led by Fernando Soto Rojas that operated around Machurucuto, on the Venezuelan Caribbean coast.

Although the men had been training for months, the weather was poor the day they landed. One of their boats capsized, causing one of the Cubans to drown. The next day, local fishermen discovered the abandoned boat and the body, reporting it to the authorities shortly after. When weapons were found aboard, the Army was mobilised to the area. By midnight of 10 May, the guerrillas were being tracked by government forces. A manhunt and subsequent battle ensued, ending with nine militiamen dead, two Cubans captured, and only one on the run, who joined Soto Rojas' group three months later. The Army is not known to have suffered any casualties.

Although the Cuban government denied any involvement in the operation, one of the prisoners revealed all the details of the operation to his captors. Also, for the Venezuelan government, the presence of North Korean-made Type 58 and Czechoslovak-made vz.58 assault rifles in the hands of the guerrillas pointed directly at Cuba. Coincidentally, as the manhunt was ongoing on land, at sea, just off the Venezuelan Caribbean coast, the submarine ARV *Carite* spotted the Soviet-flagged tug *Gromovoy*, which was in Venezuelan waters without permission. It remains unclear if its presence was related to the Cuban operation.

It was not until 1969, when Rafael Caldera was sworn in as president, that a serious policy of pacification was set in motion by the government. The *PCV* was legalised that year, and the *FALN* were officially dissolved in February. However, splinter groups continued to operate until the late-1980s under the command of two new far-left groups founded by people that were disillusioned by the new path chosen by the *PCV*, one of them was *Bandera Roja* (Red Flag) and the other the *Partido de la Revolución Venezolana* (Party of the Venezuelan Revolution). Their actions were, nevertheless, insignificant if compared to those carried out in the 1960s.

3
CIVILIAN CONTROL OF THE ARMED FORCES

The fall of Pérez Jiménez marked the end of Venezuela's ambitions to recover the land taken by its neighbours. However, the country was now facing a new challenge as a consequence of its alignment with the United States during the Cold War: stopping the spread of Cuba's influence through the region. The potential enemy was not the British Army anymore, but irregular groups that threatened internal order.

As result of the new operational prospect the *FAN* was now facing, during the 1960s weapon purchases were reduced, when compared to the previous decade, as the government considered the defence budget was too high.[1] Projects that were planned to be executed in the 1958–63 period were scrapped, among which was the acquisition of an aircraft carrier from the United States and the construction of another one in Venezuela.

Build-up of the 1960s

In 1962, the *FAV* received its first jet trainers in the form of 15 BAC Jet Provost Mk.52s. These would be the transition stage between the T-6 Texan and the T-34 Mentor – 41 of which had been acquired in 1959 – and the two-seat Vampire.

Another major purchase was made in 1965, when the *FAV*, through a program called *Ventura*, bought 74 second-hand F-86Ks from the German *Luftwaffe*. The acquisition was prompted by the increased presence of Cuban MiGs in the Caribbean. The K variant was not highly appreciated by *FAV* personnel because they usually had overheating issues with the afterburner. After the deliveries of the interceptors, the gradual process of retiring the Vampires from frontline units began.

The K variant acquired by Venezuela could be armed with two air-to-air missiles, namely the AIM-9B Sidewinder; something that was never done during their service with the *Luftwaffe*. While the Sabres were being delivered, the *FAV* placed an order for 100 of the aforementioned variant of the Sidewinder, 10 of which were training dummies. However, while the original plan was to equip the Ks with the new missiles, this was never carried out and the weapons remained stored for years.

Reorganisation of the *FAV*

In 1961, a deep restructuring process was started in the *FAV*. It aimed at providing the Air Force with an adequate structure for the new challenges it would face. New airbases were established, both on the Caribbean coast, in the north of the country, where interceptors and fighters were usually based; and inland, where bombers were closer to the areas where anti-insurgency operations commonly took place.

Airbases General José Antonio Anzoátegui, in Barcelona, and Teniente Vicente Landaeta Gil, in Barquisimeto, had been established by 1965 as part of the reform. The following decade saw further expansion of the Air Force infrastructure, with the establishment of the following bases: Mayor Buenaventura Vivas, in Santo Domingo del Táchira; General en Jefe Rafael Urdaneta, in Maracaibo; Capitán Manuel Ríos, in El Sombrero; and Teniente Coronel Luis Apolinar Méndez, in Puerto Ordaz. Although at the beginning some of these sites were used mainly for forward deployments, over the next decade active units would be based in them.

The reform also affected the organisation of the operational units. Squadrons of similar nature were all gathered in air groups. Institutions for continued formation of the human resources were also established as part of the reform, giving birth to the *Escuela Superior de la FAV*,[2] focused on the formation of fighter pilots, and the *Escuela Técnica de la FAV*,[3] which trained ground personnel and mechanics. By 1967, the *FAV* was organised as shown in Table 1. Combat aircraft were now concentrated in central and western Venezuela, focusing their firepower on protecting the Caribbean coast from naval incursions sponsored by the Cubans, and the Colombian-Venezuelan border, as at the time the Colombian Civil War had already begun and the Venezuelan government feared increased cooperation between insurgent groups from both countries.

An F-86K of the Venezuelan Air Force. All 74 fighter-bombers of this type were acquired second-hand from the German *Luftwaffe*. This example crashed on 30 April 1973, killing the pilot. (Albert Grandolini Collection)

Table 1: *FAV* Order of Battle (ORBAT), 1967

Unit	Aircraft	Base
Comando Aéreo de Combate		
Grupo Aéreo de Caza 12		
Escuadrón de Caza 34	Venom, F-86K	El Libertador AB, Maracay
Escuadrón de Caza 35	Vampire, F-86K	El Libertador AB, Maracay
Escuadrón de Caza 36	F-86F	El Libertador AB, Maracay
Escuadrón de Mantenimiento 37		El Libertador AB, Maracay
Grupo Aéreo de Bombardeo 13		
Escuadrón de Bombardeo 38	Canberra	Landaeta Gil AB, Barquisimeto
Escuadrón de Bombardeo 39	Canberra	El Libertador AB, Maracay
Escuadrón de Bombardeo 40	B-25J	Landaeta Gil AB, Barquisimeto
Escuadrón de Mantenimiento 137		El Libertador AB, Maracay
Comando Aéreo de Transporte y Reconocimiento		
Grupo Aéreo de Transporte 6		
Escuadrón de Transporte 1	C-47, C-54	Francisco de Miranda AB, Caracas
Escuadrón de Transporte 2	C-123B	Francisco de Miranda AB, Caracas
Destacamento Aéreo Especial	A65-80 Queen Air	Francisco de Miranda AB, Caracas
Escuadrón de Mantenimiento 67		Francisco de Miranda AB, Caracas
Grupo Aéreo de Reconocimiento y Enlace 1		
Escuadrón de Reconocimiento	S-51, S-55, Bell 47G	Landaeta Gil AB, Barquisimeto
Escuadrón de Enlace	AT-7, AT-11, C-45	Landaeta Gil AB, Barquisimeto
Escuadrón de Mantenimiento		Landaeta Gil AB, Barquisimeto
Comando Aéreo de Instrucción		
Escuela de Aviación Militar	T-6	Mariscal Sucre AB, Boca de Río
Grupo Aéreo de Entrenamiento 14		
Escuadrón de Vuelo Primario 141	VT-34	Mariscal Sucre AB, Boca de Río
Escuadrón de Vuelo Primario 142	Jet Provost Mk.52	Mariscal Sucre AB, Boca de Río
Escuadrón de Mantenimiento 147		Mariscal Sucre AB, Boca de Río
Escuela Superior de la FAV		Fuerte Tiuna, Caracas
Escuela Técnica de la FAV		Campo de Aviación, Maracay

Venezuela acquired 15 BAC Jet Provost T.Mk 51s from 1962. All were left in high-speed silver overall but had large surfaces on the rear fuselage and the outsides of the wing-tip-mounted drop tanks painted in dayglo orange. (Albert Grandolini Collection)

One of 21 C-123B Providers (serial 1323) acquired for the *FAV* from 1962, seen here disgorging paratroopers. This example was withdrawn from service in 1966. (Albert Grandolini Collection)

The Growth of the Army

The Army was the branch that underwent the deepest changes during the 1960s as it was the main force used against the guerrillas. As insurgent activity increased, the Ministry of Defence decided to create COIN units known as *Batallones de Cazadores*.[4] The first was the *Batallón de Cazadores José Antonio Páez*, created in 1963, with 13 of these units established by 1967. Considered part of the special forces, the members were trained by American personnel in Venezuela, the United States and Panama. Over the time, the knowledge acquired by the US Army in Vietnam was passed to this Venezuelan units.

Also, starting in 1961, a general reorganisation process of the Army was set in motion. Different units that until then operated independently were grouped into six divisions, each one covering a portion of the country. One of them, the *5ta División de Infantería de Selva* (5th Division of Jungle Infantry), headquartered in Ciudad Bolívar, was the direct precursor of the *Cazadores* in the sense that it was specifically trained to fight in jungle environment.

The few purchases for the Army during this decade consisted mainly of light armoured vehicles. In 1963, 15 amphibious FMC M59 APCs were delivered as part of a military aid program by the United States. However, the Army quickly rejected the vehicles arguing that at the time they were focusing on activating more *Cazadores* units. Despite its amphibious capabilities, the *Infantería de Marina* did not show interest in the vehicles either, as the propulsion system was deemed too complex and expensive to operate. Finally, the M59s were handed to the *Policía Aérea* (Aerial Police), the group in charge of protecting airbases of the *FAV*, where their service was relatively short, being retired less than a decade later.

Expansion of the Navy

The fact that the new potential enemy could almost exclusively arrive from the sea meant that the Navy would have to increase its amount of light and patrol ships. Thus, in 1960, they received 12 second-hand PC-461-class submarine chasers which had served with the US Navy during the Second World War. These were meant to replace the 83-foot patrol boats acquired in 1945. Before being handed to the Venezuelan Navy, the ships were overhauled at various locations. One of them, the ARV *Mejillón* (ex USS *Larchmont*), had a remarkable participation in both the *Porteñazo* and the Machurucuto incidents.

The year before, in 1959, the Venezuelan Navy also received four LSM-1-Class LSMs from the US Navy. The new ships were named ARV *Los Monjes*, ARV *Los Roques*, ARV *Los Frailes* and ARV *Los Testigos*.

Another important development was the delivery of Venezuela's first submarine, the Balao-class ARV *Carite* (ex USS *Tilefish*), on 23 July 1960. Although the deal made with the United States included two submarines, the delivery of the second ship, which was scheduled for 1962, was cancelled due to conflicts within the Venezuelan admiralty.

In 1962, the Navy took delivery of its first aircraft, a Cessna 310. The following year, two more were received. Until that moment, aircraft serving the Navy were property of both the Army and the *FAV*. Through the decade that followed, new aircraft, among which were a pair of Douglas DC-3, were handed to the Naval Aviation.

In general terms, by mid-1960s, the *FAN* had a manpower of approximately 28,500 men, divided between the Army (14,500), the Navy (5,300, of which 2,400 were marines), the *FAV* (2,800) and the National Guard (6,000).[5]

4 RUPUNUNI REBELLION AND BORDER DISPUTES

In the late 1960s and the early 1970s, a series of situations in which Venezuela was directly involved evidenced the poor operational capability of the *FAN*. These included the Rupununi Rebellion and border disputes with Colombia, Brazil and Guyana. By 1970, the *FAN*, had roughly 43,000 men, being smaller than the armed forces from other countries of comparable size, like Colombia and Peru.[1]

In addition to this, Soviet support for Cuba had given the *Defensa Anti-Aérea y Fuerza Aérea Revolucionaria* (*DAAFAR*, Revolutionary Air and Air Defence Force) the upper hand in the Caribbean. In mid-September 1962, 40 MiG-21F-13s, six MiG-15UTIs and one Yak-12 of the 32nd Guards' Fighter Aviation Regiment of the Soviet Air Force secretly arrived in Cuba in advance of the looming Missile Crisis. Once the confrontation between both major powers was solved, the Soviets decided to hand over to the Cubans the equipment they had brought in. Shortly after, Moscow provided the PF variant of the Fishbed to the *DAAFAR*. From then, and until 1970, Cuba received the PFM, PFMA, U, MF, UM and R variants of the MiG-21 in different numbers.

At the same time, Venezuela, whose government desired to recover the status of dominant regional power that the country enjoyed during the 1950s,[2] relied on the obsolete Vampires, Venoms and Sabres to defend its airspace.

The decrease in insurgent activity led to a reconsideration of the defence requirements of the country, contemplating once again a conflict with a regular force. Thus, in 1969, newly elected president Rafael Caldera launched a general modernisation program for the entire *FAN* for which the government spent over $430 million between 1971 and 1974 just on armament, mainly from France, West Germany and the United States.[3]

Increased tensions with Colombia over the Guajira Peninsula and Los Monjes Archipelago led to a stagnation of relations between both countries. Venezuelan officials had stated multiple times that they would not allow Colombia to develop military superiority over Venezuela in a moment where a war was considered very likely.[4] Despite the Venezuelan material superiority, both countries embarked upon a small arms race.

Mirages

The *FAV* had been looking for a replacement for its F-86s since at least 1969. Various options were considered, among which were the Saab J-35 Draken, the BAe Lighting and the McDonnell Douglas F-4 Phantom II, which was the ideal candidate for Venezuelan officials. However, when the United States refused to provide the Phantoms, the *FAV* turned to France, which had been marketing its Mirage fighters in Latin America recently.

The first of 10 Mirage IIIEV interceptors acquired for the *FAV* (serial number 0624) reached Venezuela in May 1973. This jet was written off in a crash on 19 October 1990. (Albert Grandolini Collection)

The four Mirage 5V fighter-bombers were acquired for air-to-ground operations. Their primary armament were unguided rockets and bombs including the Mk.81 and Mk.82, with seven of the latter seen here in front of the aircraft. (Albert Grandolini Collection)

In late-1971, Venezuela placed an order for 16 Dassault aircraft in the form of 10 Mirage IIIEVs interceptors, four Mirage 5Vs for ground attack operations, and two Mirage 5DV twin-seater trainers. Deliveries to the *FAV* were finished in late 1973. The new aircraft were operated by the *Escuadrón de Caza 33* and *34*, which belonged to the newly created *Grupo Aéreo de Caza 11*, based in El Libertador Airbase.

Along with the planes, France offered the Matra R.530 air-to-air missile, which was turned down by the *FAV*, since the Mirages could only carry one. Instead, the AIM-9Bs bought in the late-1960s, one of which could be fitted under each wing of the aircraft, was selected. Even though the decision was made before the planes were delivered, the installation of the weapon system did not occur until the late-1970s.

Canadian Freedom Fighters

As negotiations for the Mirages developed, the Venezuelan Air Force was also evaluating the possible purchase of around 20 Canadair CF-5A/Ds from the Canadian Air Force since at least 1969, after the United States refused to provide new fighters in the late-1960s.[5] Finally, in November 1971, 16 single-seater CF-5As and a pair of CF-5D two-seaters were ordered by the Venezuelans. Deliveries started on 17 February 1972 and were completed by 11 June of the same year. The Freedom Fighters were meant to replace the Vampire, Venom and the F-86F. Later, in 1974, two additional brand-new two-seaters were delivered.

The arrival of the CF-5s finally gave the *FAV* a platform to deploy the Sidewinders that had been acquired almost a decade before. Shortly after, when the first missiles were tested, the installation of the system in the Mirages started. The process, however, was slow, and it took approximately two years to have the French planes ready to use the AIM-9Bs.

With less than a decade of service in the *FAV*, the Freedom Fighters received their first upgrades, which saw the installation of new communication and navigation systems. From then on, the designation was changed to VF-5, with the A variant assigned to single-seaters, the B to the two-seaters, and RVF-5A to the reconnaissance planes.

Buckeyes and Broncos

The Jet Provost acquired in 1962 had been deemed obsolete by 1970 and a procurement program for a replacement was started. In February 1972, the *FAV* placed an order for 12 North American T-2D Buckeyes, with deliveries starting on 27 June 1973. The planes of this first batch bore the same red and white paint scheme used by

A pair of CF-5As destined for Venezuela seen shortly before their delivery to the *FAV* in 1972. The jet in the foreground (serial 6719) was one of several destroyed on the ground at Barquisimeto AB during the coup of 27 November 1992. (Albert Grandolini Collection)

Another of the Canadair-built CF-5As, seen equipped with the so-called 'dart' used for aerial gunnery practice. (Albert Grandolini Collection)

the Buckeyes of the US Navy and were assigned to a second, newly created training squadron of the *EAM*. A second batch was ordered in 1977, and this new aircraft finally replaced the Jet Provost. The second batch of Buckeyes was easily distinguishable from the first ones as it bore a camouflage pattern.

As part of the modernisation program, the *FAV* was also looking for a replacement for its B-25s, which had been used as COIN aircraft since the early-1960s. In 1972 an order for 16 brand-new Rockwell OV-10E Broncos was placed, and the aircraft delivered by the end of the following year.

After 1977, the government decided that it would increase the *FAV*'s air to ground capabilities, and a new acquisition program for such a platform was started. Besides the Bronco, Venezuelans were also evaluating the Fairchild Republic A-10 Thunderbolt II.[6] Eventually, the propeller aircraft was chosen, and a second batch of 18 second-hand OV-10As was placed in 1990. The reason given for the decision was the versatility of the Bronco when compared with the A-10, as well as the homogenisation of the fleet.

The transport fleet was also upgraded. In 1970, an order for six Lockheed C-130H Hercules was placed, with deliveries starting on 25 March 1972. These came to reinforce the fleet C-123Bs that had been delivered to the *FAV* in 1957 and replace the approximately 20 C-47s that had been delivered starting in 1947.

The *Policía Aérea* had its M59 APCs replaced with approximately 10 Israeli-built IAI/RAMTA RBY Mk.1 light armoured reconnaissance vehicles at the end of the decade.

Heavy Gear for the Army

The modernisation of the Army – and the *Infantería de Marina* – was characterised by the number of armoured vehicles it included. In all, between 1969 and 1975, over 300 vehicles including tanks, self-propelled artillery, APCs (amphibious and non-amphibious) and specialised vehicles like mobile command centres and ambulances, of various types were delivered to Venezuela.

Among the first deliveries of the program, back in 1969, were 33 Cadillac Gage V-100 Commandos that were assigned to the *Grupo de Caballería Ambrosio Plaza*. Later in the decade, an unspecified number of V-100s and V-150s were delivered. By the end of the decade, however, 58 vehicles of both versions were operational with various units.

A pair of OV-10Es from the first batch acquired by the *FAV* in 1972. (Albert Grandolini Collection)

One of 30 Cadillac Gage V-100s acquired for the Venezuelan Army, starting in 1969. (Albert Grandolini Collection)

One of 12 F3 155mm self-propelled howitzers acquired in the early 1970s. (Albert Grandolini Collection)

Between 1972 and 1975, the anti-air capabilities of the Army were enhanced with the delivery of 12 Panhard AML S530 SPAAGs, a version of the standard AML developed exclusively for Venezuela. At the same time, 22 M42A1 Dusters were also bought. The *FAN* was already familiar with the latter, as 12 Dusters had been in service with the *Infantería de Marina* since 1962. The Army's new Dusters were assigned to the *Grupo de Defensa Antiaérea José Félix Ribas*.

Keeping with the theme of equipment standardisation, 12 Mk F3 SPGs, equipped with 155mm cannons, were bought during the first half of the decade. The Mk F3 is based on the chassis of the AMX-13 (which the *FAN* had been operating since 1955). While the entire crew of the vehicle is composed of eight men, it can only accommodate two of them, creating the need for a support vehicle (usually an AMX-VCI) to transport the remaining six and the ammunition. Venezuela acquired approximately 50 AMX-VCIs of various versions (VTT-PC Command post, VTT-VCI Infantry fighting vehicle, VTT-PM mortar carrier, VTT-TB ambulance, VTT-LT artillery fire-control vehicle) as part of the modernisation plan.

Undoubtedly, the most remarkable acquisition in this decade were the 82 AMX-30B main battle tanks – the first of Venezuela's vehicles of this kind. The acquisition of a vehicle of this class had been planned since 1969, and different models were considered, including Germany's Leopard 1, the United Kingdom's Chieftain and Argentina's *Tanque Argentino Mediano*. The French candidate was selected because of the already existing relationship between France and Venezuela in the field of defence, as well as its maximum speed of 65 kilometres per hour and the simplicity of the Hispano-Suiza HS-110 engine that powers the AMX-30. The order also included four AMX-30D recovery vehicles.

The Venezuelan Army prioritised the modernisation of its armoured corps as a hypothetical conflict with Colombia would involve heavy clashes in Los Llanos, a region of approximately 377,800 square kilometres that is characterised by its openness. The portion of the border comprised by Los Llanos is the easiest area to cross between the two republics, most of the rest of it being located either in the Andean mountain system or in the Amazonian forest, both of which would prove difficult for the two countries to conduct military operations in.

Although throughout the 1970s Venezuela sought military hardware from various sources, the United States were by far the country's main partner in the defence area, with transactions worth almost US$145 million between 1972 and 1976. Venezuela was the third main buyer of American equipment in the region, only surpassed by Brazil and Chile, which spent US$209 and 150 million, respectively, in the same period.[7]

With all the new equipment, on 14 November 1974 it was decided to create the *Brigada Blindada del Ejército* (Armoured Brigade of the Army) part of the *4ta División de Infantería* (4th Infantry Division)[8] headquartered in Valencia. Its organisation was as listed in Table 2.

The Navy's New Destroyers

The Navy saw the capabilities of both its naval fleet and the *Infantería de Marina* enhanced with the arrival of new equipment. In Venezuela's modern military history, the Navy has traditionally been at the bottom of the list when it comes to equipment modernisation,

One of 82 AMX-30B main battle tanks acquired by Venezuela in the 1970s. At the time, they represented the most powerful vehicles of this kind in Latin America. (Albert Grandolini Collection)

with the exception being the marines, which during the first half of the 1970s experienced a considerable increase of its capabilities with the activation of artillery, communications and armoured groups.

The first half of the 1970s also saw the creation of various special forces groups in the Navy. The *Compañía de Incursores de la Armada* (Company of Raiders of the Navy) activated in 1973, and the *Unidad de Reconocimiento de la Infantería de Marina* (*URECIM*, Marine Corps' Reconnaissance Unit) activated in December 1975, were the first units of this nature in the Navy. While the former was tasked with 'performing commando operations to support other units of the Navy', the latter's mission was to 'perform security and land reconnaissance operations in order to facilitate the assault of landing forces and subsequent operations.' In 1985, both groups were merged into the *Unidad de Operaciones Especiales* (*UOPE*, Special Operations Unit).

The first equipment delivered to the *Infantería de Marina* as part of the modernisation program were 12 M42A1 Dusters, which came to replace a similar number of previous versions of the same vehicle that had been acquired in 1961. In 1974, the *Unidad de Tanques Anfibios de la Infantería de Marina* (Marine Corps' Amphibious Tanks Unit) was created with the delivery of 11 brand-new LVT-7s (Nine LVTP-7 personnel carriers, one LVTC-7 command post, and one LVTR-7 recovery vehicle) acquired from the United States.

By the start of the 1970s, the Navy's surface fleet was outdated and in a dire condition as consequence of poor maintenance. The three Nueva Esparta-class destroyers, which were the fleet's main ships, were barely operational, rarely setting sail from their home port in Puerto Cabello. Of the six Almirante Clemente-class frigates, two had been in the United Kingdom for years undergoing a modernisation process that was constantly delayed due to the Venezuelans' inability to pay on time for the works. The remaining four ships of the class were practically inoperative, in a similar condition to that of the Nueva Esparta-class. Only one ship, the submarine ARV *Carite* was fully operational as its maintenance had been prioritised by the Venezuelan admiralty.

Table 2: Armoured Brigade of the Venezuelan Army, 1974

Brigada Blindada del Ejército Venezolano	
Unit	**Equipment**
Compañía de Comando	AMX-13 VTT-PC
Batallón de Infantería Mecanizada José Antonio Anzoátegui	AMX-13 VTT-VCI
Batallón Blindado Bravos de Apure	AMX-30B
Batallón Blindado Pedro León Torres	AMX-30D
Batallón Blindado José Francisco Bermúdez	M18A1 Hellcat, M74 recovery vehicle
Grupo de Artillería de Campaña Autopropulsado Juan Jacinto Lara	AMX-13 Mle. F.3 AMX-13 VTT-LT
9no Grupo de Defensa Antiaérea	AML-530S

In addition to purchasing most of their combat vehicles abroad, Venezuelan armed forces went as far as to create their own designs using available equipment. One local modification included the installation of French-built Schneider Model 1928 37mm automatic guns on the chassis of the M3A1 half-track. (Albert Grandolini Collection)

Another local modification included the installation of the M4E1 turret of the M42A1 Duster self-propelled Bofors twin 40mm guns on the chassis of the AMX-13 light tank. (Albert Grandolini Collection)

The general modernisation plan also included the Navy, however, unlike the other branches, the acquisition process of brand-new equipment could take up to a decade in the case of naval ships. While a list of needs was handed to the Ministry of Defence between 1971 and 1972, it was necessary to reactivate the Navy's operational capability. Thus, the government turned to the United States to acquire surplus ships from the United States Navy. Two Allen M. Summer-class destroyers, USS *Beaty* and USS *Robert K. Huntington* were bought in 1972 and 1973 and incorporated in the Venezuelan Navy as ARV *Carabobo* and ARV *Falcón*, respectively. These would serve as 'transitional ships' until the six Mariscal Sucre-class frigates ordered from Italy by the government were delivered.

This 'transitional' fleet also included two Tench/Guppy-class submarines, the USS *Cubera*, delivered to the Venezuelan Navy in 1972 and renamed ARV *Tiburón*, and the USS *Grenadier*, which was delivered in 1973 and renamed ARV *Picúa*. These would be eventually replaced by two German-built Type 209A-class that were delivered in 1976 and 1977 and named ARV *Sábalo* and ARV *Caribe*, respectively. The order was originally for three submersibles but was reduced to two right before the construction of the third began. When the *Caribe* was delivered, the Balao-class ARV *Carite* was retired from active service.

The 1970s also saw a modernisation of the patrol fleet, with six British-built Vosper boats being delivered between 1974 and 1975: three Constitución-class gunboats and three Federación-class missile boats.

The following decade saw little development in the fleet, the highlight being the delivery of the six Mariscal Sucre-class frigates ordered in 1975. The Mariscal Sucre-class was a derivative of the Lupo-class designed specifically for Venezuela, the main difference between the two versions being that the Venezuelan ships had a fixed hangar for their helicopter instead of a telescopic one, and that it is equipped with an Aspide SAM system instead of the Sea Sparrow that was present in the original Italian ships. Physically, the Mariscal Sucre-class is like the Peruvian-built Carvajal-class, but in terms of electronic devices, the two were considerably different. Six ships were delivered: ARV *Mariscal Sucre*, ARV *Almirante Brión*, ARV *General Urdaneta*, ARV *General Soublette*, ARV *General Salom*, and ARV *Almirante García*. These came to finally replace the Nueva Esparta, Almirante Clemente and Allen M. Summer-class destroyers in service. Deliveries started in May 1980, with *Mariscal Sucre*, and ended in July 1982, with *Almirante García*.

Another noteworthy addition to the fleet during the 1980s were the Capana-class LSMs, ARV *Capana*, ARV *Esequibo*, ARV *Guajira* and ARV *Los Llanos*. Built in South Korea, these replaced the four LSM-1-class that had been in service since 1959. These would be reinforced by another two American-built LCUs that were delivered in 1982, ARV *La Orchila* and ARV *Margarita*.

In 1984, the *Infantería de Marina* took delivery of 40 Brazilian-built Engesa EE-11 Urutú amphibious APCs in three different versions (34 VTTR personnel carriers, three VCMD command posts, and three VCRP recovery vehicles).

Peace Delta

Starting in the late-1970s, the Caribbean Cold War started to get tense again. The Soviet influence had now spread to Grenada and Nicaragua, whose former US-aligned governments had been toppled by communists. Until 1980, Peru had also been in the Soviet sphere, although Moscow's influence was significantly weaker than in the other three socialist Latin American countries. At the same time, in Colombia, Guatemala and El Salvador various communist-leaning armed groups were fighting against US-backed governments. Venezuela was once again the United States' closest partner in their efforts to counter the Soviet/Cuban influence in the Caribbean.

In June 1978, Cuba's *DAAFAR* took delivery of 13 MiG-23BNs and two MiG-23UBs. A second batch of 14 BNs was delivered in early-1982. This acquisition set off all the possible 'alarm bells' in Washington to the north, as well as in Caracas, because it was widely perceived to be giving the government in Havana the upper hand in the Caribbean once again. Furthermore, shortly after the overthrowing of the Somoza regime in Nicaragua, in July 1979, the new Sandinista government asked the Soviet Union for MiGs, and ground facilities to enable the operation of the aircraft started to be built in various parts of the country.[9]

As soon as the information about the new Cuban fighters became public, the Venezuelan government started to look for an aircraft to counter them. Various options were considered, among which were the French Dassault Mirage 50 and 2000, the Israeli IAI Kfir C2, the European Panavia Tornado, the Swedish Saab J-37 Viggen and the American Northrop F-20 and General Dynamics F-16.

One of 18 F-16As acquired by the *FAV* under Project Peace Delta. (Albert Grandolini Collection)

After a thorough evaluation process of each model, the F-16 was chosen in 1980. However, Jimmy Carter's Presidential Directive 13 forbade the sale of military equipment to Latin America. While this initially threatened Venezuela's intention to acquire the Fighting Falcon, Reagan's administration made an exception and approved the sale.

The acquisition program was named Peace Delta. Initially, the *FAV* was looking for 72 aircraft, a number that was later reduced to 48, then to 36, and finally to 24 as a consequence of the deteriorating economic situation of Venezuela. Washington initially tried to sell the F-16/79 downgraded variant to Venezuela, but after the rejection of the model by the *FAV*, the Americans agreed to supply the F-16 Block 15 OCU. The final order, which was approved by President Reagan in July 1981, was composed of 18 F-16As and six F-16B two-seaters, which included a new version of the Sidewinder, the AIM-9P3. Deliveries started in November 1983 and were completed in November 1985.

The new Fighting Falcons were assigned to *Escuadrón de Caza 161* and *162*, part of the *Grupo Aéreo de Caza 16*, stationed in El Libertador AB in Maracay. The unit was established on 31 August 1983, shortly before deliveries started.

The purchase of the F-16 – and a few years later, in 1987, of the AIM-9L – by Venezuela was not exempt of criticism. Several Latin American countries, among which were Colombia and Guyana, criticised the move as they considered it could start a regional an arms race. In fact, shortly after the sale was confirmed, Peru expressed interest in the F-16/79,[10] but no deal was ever reached. Some criticism also originated in the United States, mainly alleging that advanced military hardware should not be provided to Third World nations, citing the Falklands War to argue that such equipment could be used against the US or its allies eventually. The administration defended the sale describing it as a protection measure for an oil-supplying friendly country.[11]

Mirages, Tucanos, Hercules, Rolands and other Goodies

The F-16s became the *FAV*'s first-line fighter, relegating the Mirages to secondary roles. The French aircraft's service in Venezuela was marked by accidents (see Appendix 3 in Volume 2) and attrition, as well as the obsolescence of its avionics only 10 years after delivery. Thus, since the early-1980s the *FAV* had been planning to upgrade the planes to the 50EV and 50DV standards, but the plan was delayed several times due to the acquisition of the F-16 and the plunge of oil prices. It was not until 1989, after increased tensions with Colombia, that the program was executed, with all the remaining Mirages in service being sent to France for the overhaul; that is: five Mirage IIIEVs, three 5Vs and two 5DVs.

Among many others, the main features of the plan included the replacement of the SNECMA Atar 9C with the more powerful Atar 9K-50, as well as the installation of Thomson-CSF Cyrano IVM3 radars, which allowed for the deployment of the newly-acquired Matra R.550 Magic 2 and the Aérospatiale AM.39 Exocet. Besides upgrading the existing aircraft, new ones were procured to replace others that had been lost, for this, three brand-new Mirage 5Ms, which were never delivered to their original buyer, the Zairean Air Force, were bought and upgraded to the 50DV standard. Work ran from 1990 to 1992.

With a growing number of combat aircraft in service, the demand for trainer aircraft increased. Since the early-1980s Brazil's Embraer had been marketing its EMB-312 Tucano trainer aircraft to countries of the region. In mid-1985, Venezuela placed an order for 32 Tucanos, 20 T-27 trainers and 12 AT-27 tactical support aircraft with deliveries starting on 14 July 1986. The versions are easily distinguishable as the former feature a silver livery, while the latter were painted in a camouflage scheme.

The T-27s were assigned to the *Escuadrón de Entrenamiento 142*, part of the *Grupo de Entrenamiento Aéreo 14*, while the AT-27s were sent to a newly activated unit, the *Escuadrón de Operaciones Especiales 152*, of the *Grupo Aéreo de Operaciones Especiales 15*, where they performed border patrol missions. The AT-27s would be transferred to the *Grupo de Bombardeo 13* in 1991, after the last Canberras were retired.

Transport capabilities were also enhanced. By the early-1980s, the *FAV*'s freight fleet was composed of the C-130s that had been bought in the previous decade and the C-123s that had been in service since 1957. It was decided that the Providers had to be replaced. While the Hercules was the initial candidate, it was too big to land on unpaved and improvised runways deep in the Venezuelan Amazon. This situation led the *FAV* to evaluate the Alenia G.222, two of which had been in service with the Army's air arm since 1983 and were frequently used to fly replacement troops to isolated villages in the jungle. Finally, an order for six aircraft was placed,

One of two Mirage 5DD two-seat conversion trainers acquired by the *FAV*, seen in the 1980s following an overhaul in France. (Photo by Jean-Marie Lipka)

A Mirage 5D seen prior to conversion to the Mirage 50EV standard. Notable are the R.550 Magic air-to-air missile (outboard underwing pylon), a drop tank that also served as a multiple ejector rack for Mk.81 (shown in this photograph) and Mk.82 bombs, and an AM.39 Exocet anti-ship missile. In reality, the Exocet could not be deployed from this variant, only from the later Mirage 50EV, yet was installed on this jet for the purpose of the display. (Albert Grandolini Collection)

A rare photograph from the 1980s, showing most of the *FAV*'s Mirage-fleet at once, including five Mirage IIIEVs and two Mirage 5Vs – all led by a single Mirage 5DD (third jet from the left). In the late 1980s and early 1990s the surviving Mirages were all upgraded to the Mirage 50EV standard. (Albert Grandolini Collection)

Due to geopolitical rivalry, repeated diplomatic disagreements, and differences over the demarcation of their mutual border, Colombia was seen as the most likely external enemy Venezuela might face in a war. With most of the border area being covered by savannah, from the 1940s Venezuela began prioritising and building-up its armoured force. One of the first related acquisitions came in the form of 15 M8 Greyhound armoured cars obtained from the USA. Armed with a 37mm gun and a .50-cal/12.7mm Browning machine gun, these never saw any action against Colombia but were deployed during several instances of political unrest at home. (Artwork by David Bocquelet)

Searching for a simple and reliable self-propelled anti-aircraft weapon, in the 1940s the Venezuelan Army mounted 13.2mm Hotchkiss Mle 1930 anti-aircraft machine guns on old Ford 4x4 Model 1934 trucks. A decade later, after acquiring a number of US-made M3A1 half-tracks, the Venezuelans removed their armoured passenger compartment and installed the French 37mm Schneider Model 1928 automatic gun with a simple armoured plate on the front, thus obtaining a large number of self-propelled anti-aircraft and fire-support weapons. (Artwork by David Bocquelet)

Following further differences with Colombia, in the 1950s Venezuela bolstered its armoured force though the acquisition of 40 French-built AMX-13M51s (also known as 'AMX-13V'). While lightly armoured (only 40mm on the front, with 10mm on the sides), these were armed with the high-velocity 75mm SA 50 L/61 gun with automatic loader and carried 12 rounds in the drum magazine on the rear of the turret. The Venezuelans were highly satisfied with AMX-13s, and another batch of 31 – this time of AMX-13s armed with the 90mm gun – was acquired in 1991, while some 36 of the older examples were upgraded through the installation of the same weapon. Vehicles retaining their dark blue-green overall livery as of 1992, belonged to the original batch of AMX-13Vs. (Artwork by David Bocquelet)

The success of the AMX-13 encouraged the Venezuelans to also acquire between 12 and 20 examples of the Canon de 155 mm Mle F3 Automoteur (or Mk F3) self-propelled 155mm howitzers from France. This is the smallest and lightest motorised gun carriage for 155mm artillery ever produced. The F3 howitzer is mounted on the chassis of the AMX-13 light tank, crewed by two, weighing just 18 tonnes when fully loaded. Its maximum effective range is 20,050m with 43.75kg high-explosive rounds, but it can also fire smoke, illumination, and rocket assisted shells. (Artwork by David Bocquelet)

The third armoured vehicle of the Venezuelan Army based on a French chassis is the local modification known as the AMX-13M51 Ráfaga. Essentially, this is the M-4E1 turret of the M42A1 Duster self-propelled gun, armed with two 40mm Bofors automatic cannons, installed on the chassis of the AMX-13 light tank. The Ráfaga came into being at the same time as the upgrade of surviving AMX-13M51s through the installation of the 90mm gun, and at least 10 were manufactured in total. (Artwork by David Bocquelet)

The Thyssen Henschel UR-416 was a German-made, wheeled armoured personnel carrier – based on the chassis of a Mercedes-Benz U1100 Unimog 416 truck – manufactured from 1969. The Venezuelan National Guard acquired 20 of them in 1973. Operated by several mobile detachments (for example, No. 51), they saw widespread deployment during the two coup attempts of 1992. As far as is known, most were left in dark green overall, and wore a large roundel with the title *Guardia Nacional* on the forward hull. Many were armed with a pintle-mounted 7.62mm Browning M1919 machine gun, as illustrated here. (Artwork by David Bocquelet)

Having developed defence cooperation with France over several decades, in the early 1970s Venezuela opted to acquire its first modern main battle tank from the same source. Issued in 1972, the initial order was for 142, but this was reduced to 82, plus four AMX-30Ds. In the mid-1980s, Venezuelan AMX-30s underwent a comprehensive upgrade, including the installation of the Continental AVDS-1790-5A diesel engine and new fuel tanks (stretching the range to 720km), while firepower was improved through the adoption of the Landsadot Mk I fire-control system and ballistic computer made by Elbit Systems. (Artwork by David Bocquelet)

Because of the long distances its armoured forces were expected to have to travel in the event of a conflict with one of its neighbours, the Venezuelan Army sought to acquire fast but light tanks and enable its units to wage high-mobility warfare. When the time came to replace the first generation of AMX-13s, in 1988 Caracas opted to buy a total of 78 British-made Alvis FV101 Scorpion 90s (together with four or five FV104 Samaritans, two FV105 Sultans, and four FV106 Samsons). All were delivered by 1992 (bar the Samaritans destroyed by fire en route). The primary armament of the Scorpion 90 was the long-barrelled 90mm Cockerill Mk 3 M-A1 gun, while a 7.62mm L7 general purpose machine gun was installed coaxially. (Artwork by David Bocquelet)

Through the 1970s and 1980s, the Venezuelan Army purchased a total of 30 Cadillac Gage Commando V-100s, and 100 V-150s. While the V-100 is relatively lightly armed and primarily serves as an armoured personnel carrier, the latter – shown here – has the same dimensions but is reinforced to enable the carrying of heavier weapons systems, such as large smoothbore guns for fire-support and anti-tank purposes – such as the 90mm Cockerill Mk 3 cannon. Other armament can include up to two 7.62mm machine guns and grenade launchers. While up to 39 rounds of 90mm ammunition can be stored inside the hull, the vehicle still offers enough space for four passengers, in addition to the crew of three. (Artwork by David Bocquelet)

Among the first responders to the presence of rebel troops in Caracas were members of the *Guardia Nacional* (National Guard). Their regular uniform consisted of a khaki shirt and dark green pants. Because of the nature of their usual task, mostly consisting of policing, they usually lacked heavy armament. Therefore, in February 1992, the *Guardia Nacional* gathered whatever gear – including ballistic vests – they could find before moving out to engage the rebels, who they knew were superior in firepower. Depicted here is a member of the *Guardia Nacional* in regular uniform and wearing a helmet equipped with a visor, as typically used in riot control duties. (Artwork by Anderson Subtil)

A typical infantry soldier of the Venezuelan Army as of the early 1990s wore a uniform based on the US-made M81 Battle Dress Uniform (BDU; also known as the Camouflage Utility Uniform, CUU) with Gore-Tex Parka and trousers in the four-colour (sand, green, brown, and black) disruptive Woodland camouflage pattern. A locally-manufactured FN FAL assault rifle was the regular issue personal weapon, and the AT-4 light anti-tank weapon was frequently distributed to both loyalist and rebel troops, being common during both coups of 1992. (Artwork by Anderson Subtil)

Based on the M81 BDU uniform in Woodland pattern, the appearance of the *Paracaidista* (paratroopers) of the Venezuelan Army was generally similar to that of the infantry. The primary difference was their red berets and – to improve identification friend or foe – armbands in Venezuelan national colours, as shown here. (Artwork by Anderson Subtil)

Together with the *Guardia Nacional*, the *Policía Metropolitana de Caracas* (Metropolitan Police of Caracas) was one of first branches to resist the rebel presence in the capital. Of course, as the loyalist forces became better organised and started coordinating its responses, it returned to the role of the police. Depicted here is a police officer wearing a shirt in light olive green and blue trousers, topped by the regular riot gear of a vest and helmet, and armed with a pump-action shotgun and service pistol. (Artwork by Anderson Subtil)

Selected patches of the major branches and units of the Venezuelan Army and other security agencies, including (from left to the right, and line by line): 42nd Parachute Infantry Brigade; 421st Parachute Infantry Battalion *José Leonardo Chirinos*; Caracas Metropolitan Police; Fuerte Tiuna; Presidential Honour Guard; Scientific, Penal and Criminalistic Investigation Service Corps (*CICPC*, then called *PTJ*); 11th Infantry Brigade; and 1st Infantry Division. (Artworks by Anderson Subtil)

Comparison of national insignia of the Venezuelan Air Force, with those of Ecuador and Colombia. (Artwork by Tom Cooper)

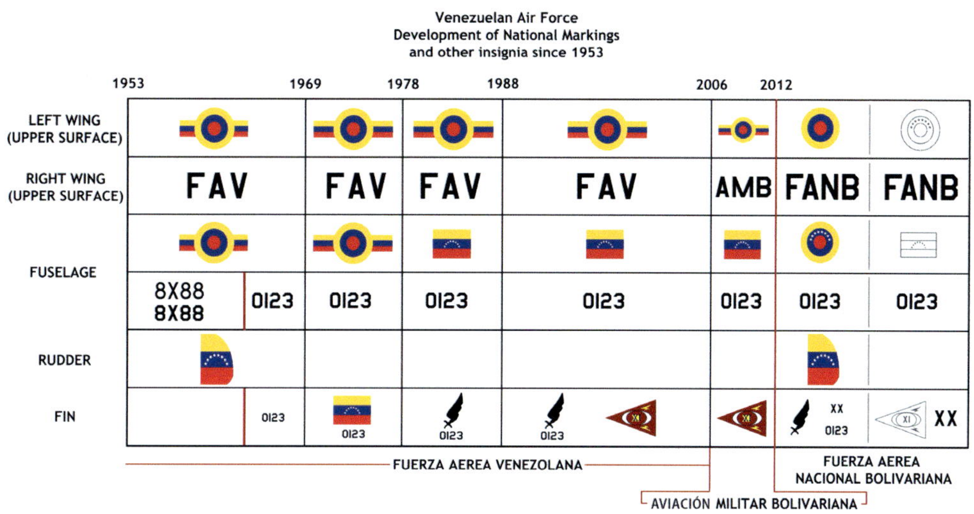

Development of the national insignia, application of serial numbers and service titles of the *FAV*, *Aviación Militar Bolivariana* and the *Fuerza Armada Nacional Bolivariana*, since 1953. (Diagram by Tom Cooper)

While searching for a new training aircraft, in 1959 Venezuela opted for Beechcraft T-34A Mentor and placed an order for a total of 41. Most entered service with the *Grupo Aéreo de Entrenamiento 14* of the *FAV*, serving as basic trainers, being replaced by SF.260s from 2000. Ten examples were assigned to the *Grupo Aéreo de Entrenamiento 14*. All were always painted in silver-grey overall and wore red fuselage bands and red wingtips, with the letter 'E' denoting them as training aircraft. Originally, the 'E' was followed by serials from 001 to 0041, but in 1966, and like all other *FAV* aircraft, they received new, random four-digit serial numbers. (Artwork by Tom Cooper)

In 1985, Venezuela acquired 32 Embraer Tucanos in two versions: 20 T-27 for training purposes, and 12 AT-27 for counterinsurgency purposes. The training aircraft sported a silver paint scheme, with a red fuselage band and a large white letter 'E' on each side, and could be armed with machine gun pods, or pods for unguided rockets. Both T-27s and AT-27s served on both sides during rebellions of 1992: some were tasked by government forces with bombing the *Museo Histórico Militar* in Caracas; and then as part of the rebel-operated fleet that attacked multiple targets along the Valencia-Maracay-Caracas axis. With the type having no internally-installed armament, the primary weapon became FN ETNA-HMP pods containing a 12.7mm machine gun, one of which was carried under each wing. (Artwork by Tom Cooper)

Together with OV-10s, AT-27s – like this example with serial number 7321 – have been extensively used in the western part of the country, both against Colombian guerrillas and cartel-operated light aircraft. Combined with the lack of protective facilities, this regularly resulted in their camouflage pattern – consisting of tan (FS30219), light green (FS34102), and dark green (FS34079) on upper surfaces and sides, and light grey (FS36622) on undersurfaces – becoming dirty, and the colours washed-out. In addition to FN ETNA-HMP pods (sometimes with the MRL 70 attached underneath: this included four tubes for 70mm unguided rockets), Venezuelan Tucanos were sometimes armed with FN ETNA TMP-5 pods for twin 7.62mm machine guns, as illustrated here. (Artwork by Tom Cooper)

In early-1972, Venezuela purchased a dozen T-2D Buckeyes to replace the aging Jet Provost that had been the backbone of the jet trainer fleet of the *FAV* since 1962. The aircraft of this first batch were based on the T-2C of the US Navy, without the capability of deploying weapons, and wearing the same white-and-orange paintjob as their North American counterparts. Five years later, in 1977, a second batch was acquired, this time based on the T-2E of the Hellenic Air Force, and with the capability to carry weapons. Aircraft from each batch were easily distinguishable based on their camouflage colours. Although assigned to the *Grupo Aéro de Caza 12*, T-2Ds were never used for counterinsurgency operations: they served as lead-in trainers along with the C/VF-5Ds of the *Escuadrón de Escuela de Combate 35*. At least six Buckeyes were operated by rebellious pilots on 27 November 1992: amongst them was the example illustrated here, serial number 7861. (Artwork by Tom Cooper)

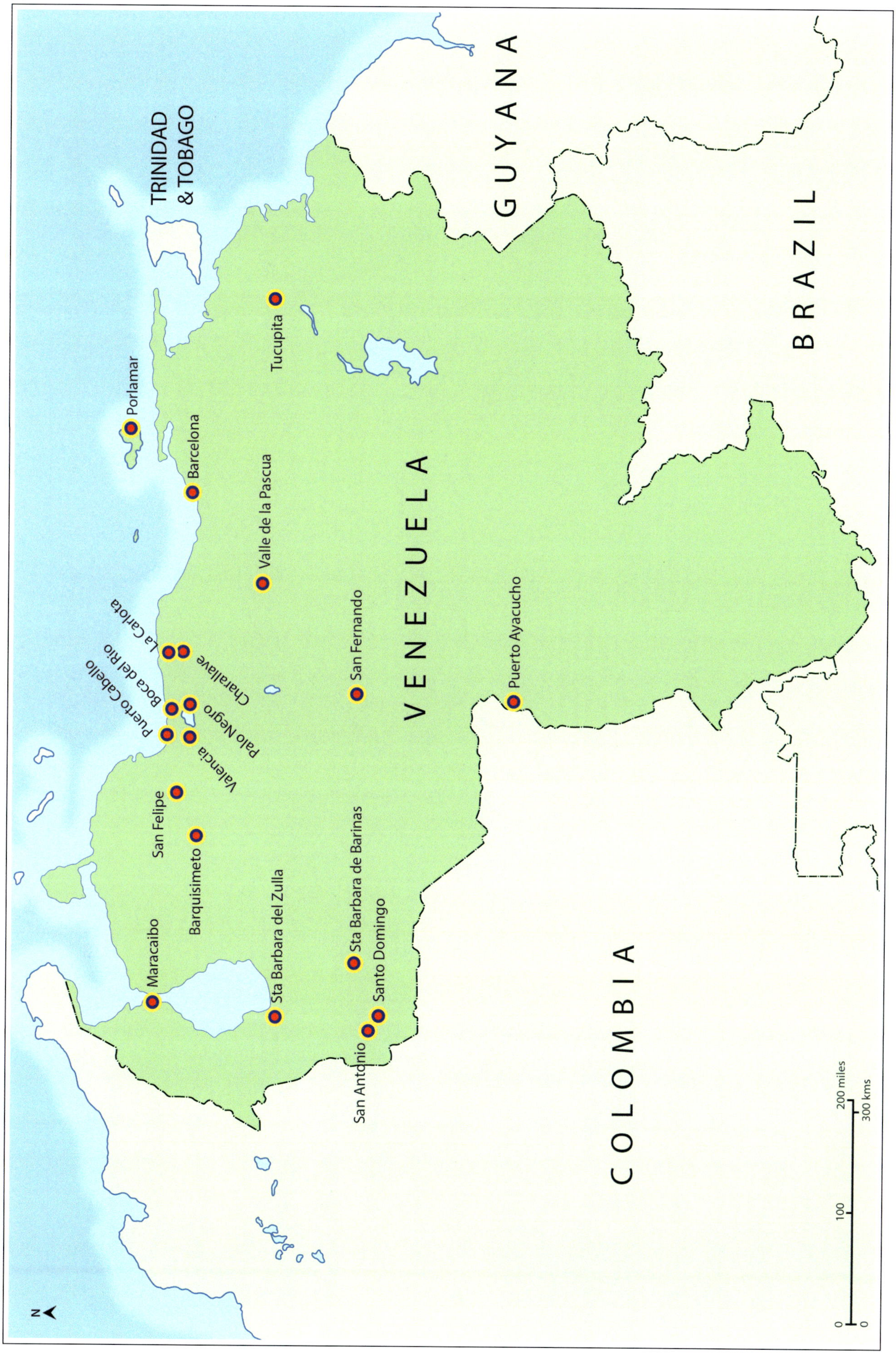

A map of Venezuela showing the major air bases of the *FAV* in 1992. (Map by Paul Hewitt)

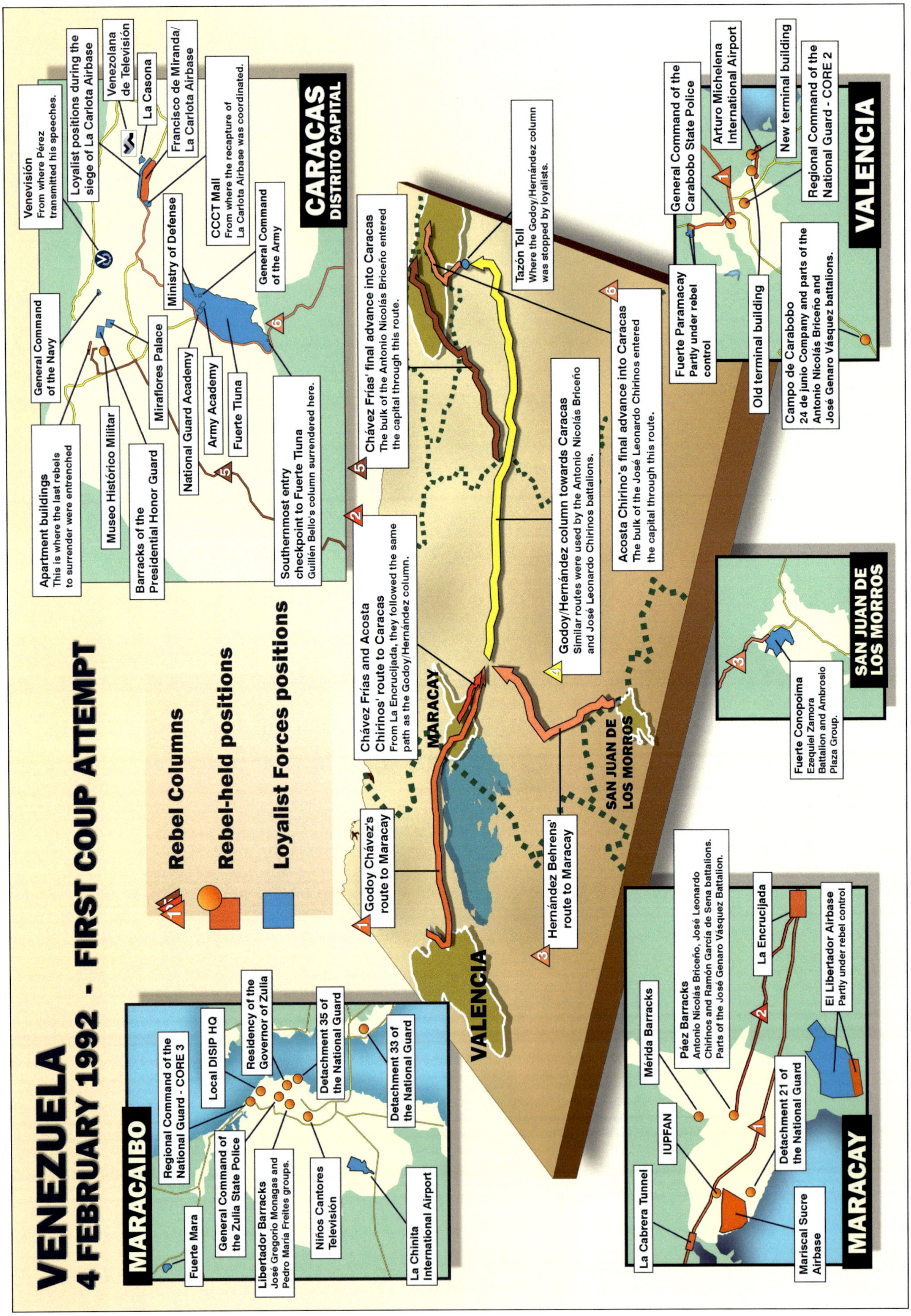

The major locations of the first coup attempt, of 4 February 1992. (Map/art by Anderson Subtil)

One of the first two Mirage 50EVs seen shortly after the conversion, during predelivery testing in France. (Albert Grandolini Collection)

A pair of AT-27s (centre) with two T-41 Mentors. (Albert Grandolini Collection)

with deliveries taking place between 1984 and 1985. The G.222 had a poor reception in the *FAV* due to its high operational cost and logistical difficulties to acquire spare parts. In consequence, their operational availability was intermittent and irregular.

The 1980s also saw the arrival of the first SAM system in Venezuela. In 1978, the *Comando de la Defensa Aérea* (Air Defence Command), reporting directly to the Ministry of Defence, was established. Between 1982 and 1984, three AAA squadrons were formed after the purchase of six Euromissile Roland 2 launchers, several Bofors 40mm L/70 and Oerlikon 20mm AA guns, and Signaal Flycatcher fire-control systems.

With the intention of strengthening the air defence net that was being established, by 1983 the *FAV* tried to acquire Airborne Early Warning and Control capabilities. The primary option was to buy two Northrop Grumman E-2 Hawkeyes from the United States, but due to financial difficulties the purchase never took place.

On 24 March 1986, the *Departamento de Búsqueda y Rescate* (Search and Rescue Department) was established. Its primary mission was to execute search and rescue operations required by the *FAV*, which often involve missing pilots and aircraft involved in accidents.

Other special forces groups were established in the 1980s, among which was the Army's *Batallón de Fuerzas Especiales Coronel Domingo Montes*, part of the 5ta *División de Infantería de Selva* since 1986. The National Guard's *Grupo de Acciones Especiales* (Special Actions Group), a counter-terrorist unit, was also formed in this decade, in June 1985.

The geopolitical situation had remained the same since the previous decade, so the Army's main acquisitions continued to be oriented to strengthening the armoured and artillery corps. In 1983, two batteries of IMI LAR-60 MLRS were acquired. The system was mounted on the modified chassis of the AMX-13. A

One of seven G.222 transports acquired by the *FAV* in the 1980s. All were non-operational by 1992. (Albert Grandolini Collection)

A row of C-130H Hercules of the *Escuadrón de Transporte T1*, seen in the late 1980s. Venezuela acquired a total of eight of these transports, and six of these were operational as of 1992. (Albert Grandolini Collection)

year later, 10 RMMV TPz Fuchs 1 were delivered and assigned to the *Batallón de Infantería Mecanizada*. In late-1986, a major order for 101 Arrowpoint Corporation Dragoon 300 AFVs was placed. The purchase included five different versions of the platform (42 Dragoon 300 VBCC combat vehicles armed with a 90mm canon, 25 VBTP personnel carriers, 21 VBPM mortar carriers, 11 VBPC command posts, and two VBR recovery vehicles). After deliveries were finished, the M18A1 Hellcats that were still in service were retired and placed in storage. Two years later, in 1991, the Yugoslav firm SPDR Arms presented the *FAN* with a prototype for a potential modernisation of the Hellcat. However, the Army turned down the offer in favour of the possibility of acquiring more AMX-30s.

After the crisis relating to the Colombian corvette ARC *Caldas* (see below), Venezuela embarked upon yet another reequipment program commonly known as the *Plan Global de Adquisiciones*. The armoured corps were once again the priority in this program. Thus, over 100 EE-11 Urutús were ordered from Brazil for the Army. However, Engesa, the manufacturing company, was bankrupt at the time and in consequence was unable to deliver the vehicles ordered by Venezuela.

France offered an undetermined number of AMX-30s that had originally been ordered by Iraq, but the Venezuelan Ministry of Defence instead chose an offer from the United Kingdom consisting of 78 Scorpion 90 light tanks, four FV106 Samson recovery vehicles, two FV105 Sultan mobile command posts and two FV104 Samaritan ambulances.[12] The light tank fleet was reinforced in 1991 when 31 second-hand AMX-13.C90s were bought from France. After deliveries were completed, the old AMX-13M51s were placed in storage.

Economic Crisis and the Caldas Incident

When the Venezuelan economy started to collapse in 1983, at first the government sought to reduce military spending, as described above. However, continuation of tensions with Colombia and resurgence

One of 31 second-hand AMX-13s with C.90 turret acquired from France in 1991. (Albert Grandolini Collection)

of armed communist insurgency forced the administration to reconsider this decision by the end of the 1980s and the beginning of the 1990s.

Although the guerrilla movements had considerably reduced their activity due to a mix of government pressure and lack of popular support, they had managed to infiltrate the officer ranks of the *FAN*. Already in 1983 there were rumours of an impending coup, although it was also palpable that most of the military was loyal to the government.[13] Finally, the takeover plan was not set in motion after the officers behind it were unable to secure popular support.

On 9 August 1987, the corvette ARC *Caldas* (hull number FM-52) of the Colombian Navy entered Venezuelan waters without permission, sparking a crisis that would last until 18 August and brought both countries to the verge of war. Through the nine days the crisis lasted, Venezuelan ships chased the Colombian Navy presence in the disputed area, eventually escalating to the point that both countries mobilised troops to the border areas. The crisis was defused when Venezuela issued an ultimatum for the Colombian ships to be called back to their ports, threatening to sink them if they stayed in Venezuelan waters.

The so-called Caldas incident made the government increase military spending again, with investment in both the acquisition of new equipment and the upgrade of war materiel already in *FAN* service. In this regard, in a similar procedure to that of the Mirages, the *FAV* set in motion a modernisation program for the VF-5s, nicknamed *Proyecto Grifo*, which was to be carried out with assistance from Singapore Technologies Aerospace, starting in 1991. Both avionics and structural changes were made, with the installation of a HUD, IFF and TACAN systems; strengthening of the wing structures; the fitting of an ALE-40 countermeasure dispenser and a refuelling probe on the right side of the aircraft, which would be needed as the *FAV* incorporated two Boeing 707-320C tankers the same year. Other changes made by other companies included the installation of the AIM-9P3 weapons system, replacing the AIM-9B, and the actualisation of the General Electric J85-CAN-15 engines.

Also, in 1991, a NF-5A and six NF-5Bs, all second-hand and made with parts manufactured by both Canadair and Fokker, were bought from the Royal Dutch Air Force. This was done to replace the aircraft lost in accidents since 1972.

La Noche de los Tanques

On 26 October 1988, a military operation whose nature has been a matter of dispute and that has been surrounded by mystery and secrecy took place. President Jaime Lusinchi was out of the country, paying an official visit to Uruguay, and the country was being led by Simón Alberto Consalvi, Minister of the Interior, while the president was travelling. Just after 19:00, Major José Domingo Soler Zambrano, second-in-command of the *Grupo de Caballería Juan Pablo Ayala*, stationed in Fuerte Tiuna (a complex that hosts, among other things, the Ministry of Defence of Venezuela and the official residence of the vice president), ordered a column of armoured vehicles to surround both the residence and the Ministry of Interior. Soon enough, the Dragoon 300 IFVs of the group were being positioned outside of the designated targets. Not understanding the nature of the presence of the vehicles outside his residence, only being told by a captain that they were there to 'provide protection for the vice president', Consalvi telephoned General Italo del Valle Alliegro, then-minister of defence. Del Valle Alliegro ordered other units of the Army to move to Fuerte Tiuna to protect the vice president and to arrest the commanders of the operation.

To this day, little information about this event is available, and the nature of the movement is not entirely known. Major Soler Zambrano was imprisoned for a few months, and the issue was rapidly forgotten due to the events of 27 February 1989.

Renewed Political Unrest

Meanwhile, the whole decade of the 1980s saw a resurgence of insurgent activity as a consequence of the economic and social crises, something that had been predicted by officials of Venezuela's main partner, the United States.[14] New groups had been formed

Colombian corvette ARC *Caldas* (FM-52), seen in rough seas in 1984. (US Navy)

in the years that followed the demobilisation of most of the *FALN*, like *Organización de Revolucionarios* (*OR*, Organisation of Revolutionaries) and *Tendencias Unificadas Para Alcanzar el Movimiento de Acción Revolucionaria Organizada* (*TUPAMARO*, Unified Trends to Reach the Organised Revolutionary Action Movement). One of the new groups also kept using the name *FALN*, however, it was linked to the *Partido de la Revolución Venezolana* (*PRV*, Party of the Venezuelan Revolution) and not the *PCV*. In addition, other groups that formed in the late stages of the conflict in the 1960s were still operational, like *Bandera Roja*.

However, unlike in the past, now most of the actions carried out by the insurgents were of partisan nature, executed by their urban cells, the *UTC*. Aerial piracy was popular in the early 1980s, the most famous case being the simultaneous hijacking of three airliners, two Douglas DC-9-50s of Aeropostal and a Boeing 727-200 of Avensa, on 5 December 1981. After a four day-long journey that took the hijacked aircraft through various Latin American countries, they finally landed in Cuba, where the terrorists were granted asylum.

A series of skirmishes in the countryside also took place, with victories for both the government and the guerrillas, with some being considered massacres after reports that the dead guerrillas were in reality farmers whose bodies had weapons planted after being shot. Almost 40 years after massacres occurred in Cantaura, El Amparo and Yumare, among others, these remain subjects of controversy.

5
27 FEBRUARY 1989; *CARACAZO*

27 February 1989 is a date that went down in the history of Venezuela as the day when the expiration of the political system established in 1958 became clear to the population. Economic measures taken by Carlos Andrés Pérez, who had been sworn as president for a second time less than four weeks before, which aimed at palliating the economic hardships the national economy, exacerbated the already-heated spirits of the population.

Early in the morning of that day, protests because of an increase in public transportation fees were reported in Guarenas and Guatire, both towns approximately 15 kilometres east of Caracas. The situation rapidly escalated into generalised looting of supermarkets and shops. The situation quickly spread to the capital, with people from the slums going to the city to protest the abandonment they had suffered from the government. The police were unable to coordinate an effective first response, which allowed the situation to turn into a looting rampage. Tensions remained high through the day, and on the 28th, similar situations were registered in other major cities of the country like La Guaira, Maracay, Valencia, Mérida, and Ciudad Guayana.

In spite of the situation, Pérez implemented martial law and suspended a number of constitutional rights, ordering the Army to step in and re-establish order by any means. Clashes between looters and military personnel took place throughout Caracas, causing a high number of casualties that remains a matter of discussion today. The situation was not entirely controlled until mid-March, leaving billions of dollars of damaged property.

The official figure says that only 276 or 277 people were killed. However, independent investigations estimate that the death toll was well above 3,000 and that many bodies were dumped in mass graves in the outskirts of Caracas. The situation in the country became increasingly tense. Civil disobedience was widespread, rioting was a daily phenomenon, and the expiration of the political model installed in 1958 was evident. The military was not exempted from this, and conspiracies started to develop in all branches.

R83/ARMA

Although the adjustment of the *FAN* into the political system between 1958 and 1962 made possible the momentaneous quelling of the praetorianism that had dominated Venezuelan politics since its independence, it did not take long for a new generation of officers with political ambitions to show up. The most relevant conspiratorial group of this new era, *Revolución 1983* (*R83*), has its roots in the early 1970s, when then-Captain William Izarra Caldera of the *FAV* started to recruit young officers that shared his dissatisfaction with the state of affairs both within the *FAN* and the country in general. Among these young officers was then-Lieutenant Francisco Efraín Visconti Osorio.

R83 was properly established in 1979, and its aim was to stage a coup in or before 1983. Before 1979, the group's activity was limited to ideological discussions, expanding its membership and contact with members of the *PRV*, a marginal, far-left political party led by former *FALN* leader Douglas Bravo, and whose membership included Adán Chávez, Hugo Chávez's brother. It is important to say that there was no organisational contact between *R83* and the *PRV*, with the former being an exclusively military group. Furthermore, not all of its members had contacts with the *PRV*, since many did not share the leftist ideals of the party.

Although the group was established by members of the *FAV*, they eventually integrated members of the Army who were in contact with the *PRV*. The party was the main source of new members, who first contacted Bravo, who in turn linked them to Izarra. The *R83* sector in the Army was led by lieutenant colonels Ramón Guillermo Santeliz Ruíz, Ramón Alexis Sánchez Paz, Emilio Arévalo Braasch, Carlos Rodolfo Santiago Ramírez and Francisco Javier Arias Cárdenas, who joined the group in 1980.

The ideological basis of *R83* as an organisation was undoubtedly leftist, but not exactly the same as that of the *PRV*. Furthermore, as mentioned before, not all members shared these ideas, which led many of them to leave the group, among which was Visconti Osorio, who left during the mid-1980s. *R83*'s main criticism was directed towards the situation of the *FAN*, which they considered was a political instrument whose leadership was plagued by corruption and cronyism. Furthermore, the *de facto* two-party system was considered detrimental to the interests of the nation. The political plans of *R83* are not known in detail, with only a general outline having been made public, as explained in Domingo Irwin's book *Militares y conspiración: De las guerras civiles a los golpes de Estado* (see bibliography).

R83 mutated into a new group, *Alianza Revolucionaria de Militares Activos* (*ARMA*, Revolutionary Alliance of the Active Military)[1] at some point in 1982–83 for unknown reasons. Citing General Fernando Ochoa Antich, Irwin says that there was a coup d'état planned for 5 July 1982, which was to be executed during the usual military parade for Independence Day. He further explains that Carlos Santiago Ramírez became hesitant shortly before, his task for the uprising being the mobilisation of the *Pedro León Torres* Battalion. The aborted operation is cited as the reason behind the group's mutation.

Izarra remained as leader of *ARMA*, assisted by Visconti Osorio and Luis Ramón Reyes Reyes (now both captains). The activities of the group remained almost unchanged, establishing contacts with other conspiratorial groups, among which was the *Movimiento Bolivariano Revolucionario 200* (*MBR-200*, Revolutionary Bolivarian Movement-200), of which Hugo Chávez was a member, and seeking international assistance. General Visconti says in his book *27N: ¡Un golpe aéreo!* that members of *ARMA* and *PRV* were in contact with the governments of Cuba, Iraq, Libya, and Nicaragua, visiting the countries on various occasions through the early-1980s after triangulating each of their trips through an Eastern European country, usually Czechoslovakia, and receiving fake Cuban passports in order to conceal their activities from the Venezuelan government.

However, by 1985 the intelligence services were already aware of the existence of *ARMA*, which ultimately led to the fragmentation of the group in 1986, when Izarra was forced to retire from the *FAV*. Various cells remained active, led by the former assistants of the previous leader, including Visconti Osorio, Reyes Reyes and Wilmar Alfredo Castro Soteldo. From retirement, Izarra tried to keep with his activities, founding the *Frente Patriótico* (*FP*, Patriotic Front) in association with various intellectuals, members of the political left and his contacts in the military that remained active. It is said that

CARACAZO

The term *Caracazo* stems from the name of Caracas and the suffix '-azo', which stems from another historic event, the *Bogotazo*, a massive riot that in 1948 completely destroyed downtown Bogota, in Colombia. As such, it can be interpreted as the 'Caracas smash'.

There had been unrest for several days with intense student demonstrations against neoliberalism. Mass protests, following by rioting, erupted in Guarenas on the morning of 27 February 1989, and then spread to Caracas and neighbouring places, as President Pérez dismissed all the warnings from various officials of his government. As far as is known, police in Caracas opened fire at the crowd around 13.00hrs and by 18.00hrs at least 65 civilians were reported as dead.

Through the morning of 28 February, hundreds of protesters spread throughout Caracas to launch vicious attacks on foreign-owned shops. Gradually, the demonstrations and rioting turned into a near revolt with the participation of almost all social groups. Only at that point in time did Pérez react – and he promptly adopted a heavy-handed approach: after declaring a state of emergency and martial law, he suspended the Constitution, declared the (predominantly) poor protesters to be subversives, and then ordered the 'neutralisation of looting' in the name of protecting private property. Ironically, while the government then went on to blame radical political groups, these were all surprised by the escalation and even busy attempting to prevent the looting. The unrest thus went on and on 1 March 1989, Army troops opened fire on a crowd in the town of Petare, killing 20 people, before engaging several radical groups in a number of firefights.

By the morning of 2 March, and despite the curfew, the streets of Caracas were littered by the bodies of those shot during the night: the majority of wealthy citizens fled the country, while many others began organising into self-defence groups. The *Caracazo* had largely subsided, and even clashes between the Army and radical groups stopped, as the latter began running out of ammunition. Tensions only eased from 4 March, when Army troops began sweeping through neighbourhoods: however, even these operations were characterised by the disproportionate application of violence, and numerous civilians were shot to death in the following days. Unsurprisingly, the Pérez administration attempted to block all related investigations for months afterwards. The rioting destroyed the majority of commercial facilities around Caracas: and food markets especially were damaged to a degree where the system of food distribution for the poor collapsed and thousands had to line up at government food distribution centres for days after. Constitutional rights were completely restored on 22 March, and an official commission was established to investigate the events, but its findings satisfied nobody. Indeed, in 1998, the Inter-American Commission on Human Rights condemned the government's action and referred the case to the Inter-American Court of Human Rights. A year after, the court found that the government had committed violations of human rights, including extrajudicial killings. However, while the government subsequently accepted the findings, only Defence Minister Italo del Valle Allegro was ever charged in relation to these events. Unsurprisingly, in the years after, the *Caracazo* resulted in severe political instability in Venezuela.

Rioters attacking the office of Carlos Andrés Pérez Rodríguez's AD party. (Albert Grandolini Collection)

Troops of the Venezuelan Army stand guard over arrested rioters in the streets of Caracas on 27 February 1989. (Albert Grandolini Collection)

A member of the National Guard forcing away a group of protesters in Caracas, early on 27 February 1989. (Albert Grandolini Collection)

A UR.416 APC of the National Guard on the streets of Caracas. The government reacted with a heavy hand to put down what was essentially a looting rampage. (Albert Grandolini Collection)

An ancient M8 armoured scout car next to two other vehicles of the National Guard, securing a crossroad in Caracas during the days-long riots of February 1989 that became known as the *Caracazo*. (Albert Grandolini Collection)

Douglas Ignacio Bravo Mora, a long-term politician and guerrilla fighter, involved in the *PCV* since the second half of the 1940s. Ideologically opposed to the policies of the USSR, but a fervent anti-imperialist, in 1980 he began recruiting military officers sympathetic to his cause. (Photo by Guillermo Ramos Flamerich)

William Izarra Caldera (here at the time with the rank of lieutenant colonel) was Bravo's primary point of contact within the *FAV*. (Mark Lepko Collection)

they even contacted former president Rafael Caldera and offered him the leadership of the country if he supported the coup. However, *FP* was a short-lived experiment that ended in failure.

Despite this, there were other groups conspiring already, among which was the *MBR-200*.

Hugo Rafael Chávez Frías and the *MBR-200*

Any effort into investigating the origin of the *MBR-200* will unavoidably lead to controversial debates about whether there were links or not between the founders of the movement and far-left political parties like the *PRV* and *Bandera Roja* at the time of its inception; and then, should the conclusion be that, indeed, there were contacts between them, the discussion would shift to the question of how close were such relationships, and whether it was the political parties exercising influence in the conspiratorial group, or vice versa.

In any case, one thing that is certain is that, by the second quarter of the 1980s, the *MBR-200* was already incorporating young officers into its ranks. This was facilitated by the fact that some of the founders of the movement were part of the staff of the Military Academy. It is also true, however, that at this point the activities of the group were limited to political discussions, and that no decision had been made regarding the execution of a coup attempt.

Among the founding officers of the *MBR-200* we find Felipe Antonio Acosta Carlez, Yoel Candelario Acosta Chirinos, Hugo Rafael Chávez Frías, Jesús Miguel Ortiz Contreras, and Jesús Ernesto Urdaneta Hernández. All five had one thing in common: they joined and graduated from the Military Academy at the same time, belonging to the class of 1975, named 'Simón Bolívar II'. It is worth mentioning that this was the first group of cadets that graduated from the *Academia Militar de Venezuela* (*AMV*, Military Academy of Venezuela) after its institutional status was raised to that of a university.[2] Because of this, members of this class were held in high regard by younger cadets through the coming years. This was a key factor in the recruitment of new members of the *MBR-200*.

Multiple sources, including Chávez himself in numerous interviews, state that, although he was influenced by leftist ideas prior to his enrolment in the *AMV*, he was not ideologically or otherwise committed to change the course of Venezuelan politics when he joined the cadet corps. He went as far as to state that he was not pursuing a career in the military when he applied to enter the *AMV*, and that he just wanted to make it to Caracas so he could get in touch with baseball scouts, because he wanted to be a professional player and there were no teams in Barinas, his home state, or in any of the neighbouring states.

The early contact with leftist ideologies was a product of friendships with local communist militants, some of whom were *FALN* sympathisers. Chávez described his ideological evolution as a long process but pointed to the influence of the Panamanian and Peruvian revolutions, led by Omar Torrijos Herrera and Juan Velasco Alvarado, respectively, as the definitive root of his convictions. Both processes were ongoing during Chávez's cadet years, and their impact was magnified by the presence of several cadets in the *AMV* from both countries through this formative period. Furthermore, in 1974, he and Ortiz Contreras were part of the Venezuelan representation for the celebration of the 150th anniversary of the Battle of Ayacucho, in Perú. They were received personally by Velasco Alvarado. Torrijos Herrera was also present for the celebrations.

After graduating, Chávez Frías was posted to the *Batallón de Cazadores* Manuel Cedeño, which was conducting counterinsurgency activities in the eastern state of Sucre. It was during his time there that Chávez started to identify with the cause of the guerrillas he was fighting against.

Also shrouded in uncertainty is how he established contact with members of the leftist political parties for the first time, although the logical link would be his brother, Adán Coromoto Chávez Frías, a professor in the *Universidad de Los Andes* and longtime communist militant, who, at the time of Chávez's graduation, was involved with the *PRV*.

It can be said that the formal establishment of the *MBR-200* was on 17 December 1982, when the first Bolivarian Oath was made by Acosta Carlez, Chávez Frías, Urdaneta Hernández and Raúl Isaías Baduel before the Samán de Güere.[3] However, General Fernando Antonio Ochoa Antich, Minister of Defence during the 4 February rebellion, argues that several years before, in 1977, Chávez and Urdaneta were already discussing the formation of a conspiratorial cell, and that they approached other officers in an attempt that would ultimately be futile, as the group was divided when its members were posted to different units on opposite sides of the country.

Less than five years later, he had been relocated to Caracas, to a teaching job in the *AMV*. Because his future co-conspirators were already posted to units stationed near-by, they soon resumed their meetings in which they discussed the overall situation of the country, as well as the internal issues of the *FAN*. Shortly after, they started studying Simón Bolívar's thoughts, after the political leanings of the movement had been decided. This was a particularly complicated issue, because, at the beginning, the leaders of *MBR-200* contacted officers regardless of their ideology, as long as they were critical of the path the country and the *FAN* were on. When it was decided that in the medium- or long-term the goal of the group was to attain political power, the necessity of choosing an ideology became evident.

Through this process it also became evident that there were deep differences between the leaders of the movement. Captain Ismael Pérez Sira, who joined the *MBR-200* in 1986, maintains that each member of the movement's leadership had, not one, but several agendas of their own, and that it was agreed that, while the movement would have leftist leanings and would cooperate with revolutionary parties, it would not officially embrace Marxism.[4] Ochoa Antich argues that one of the reasons why being openly communist would have been counterproductive for the rebels was because the memory of the insurgency of the 1960s was still fresh for the masses. Another trend that was popular among sectors of the military was *perezjimenismo*, but, as it was an eminently personalist current, it would not have received support from the potentially sympathetic sector of the population without Pérez Jiménez's explicit involvement with the rebels. Thus, it was decided to formulate a new proposal from scratch, a process whose result was *Bolivarianismo*.

For the most part, outside of the leadership of the *MBR-200* and their partners from political parties, young officers, the bulk of the *Comacates* within the movement,[5] were eminently nationalists, without a clear ideological leaning, something that caused clashes with the first group more than once.[6] One exception was Francisco Javier Arias Cárdenas, who had graduated from the *AMV* one year before the rest of the leadership. Having known Chávez since the late-1970s, he did not join the movement until the mid-1980s because of its leftist leanings. That was also the reason why his association with *R83* was short. The only demand he made when he joined *MBR-200* was that the contact with Douglas Bravo and his people should be limited, although he also had differences with Chávez on what the role of the *FAN* in the revolutionary process should be.

Young Hugo Rafael Chávez Frías as a cadet in the *AMV*. (Albert Grandolini Collection)

Five Congresses

The decade-long conspiratorial effort meant that the movement had enough time not only to absorb other groups with similar goals, but also to develop its own working dynamic. Members organised themselves in cells of not more than 10 people, and only the leader of each cell knew who the regional leader of the *MBR-200* was. This way, in case loyalists of the government found out, the information they would be able to get from those discovered would be minimal. This was the case in 1986, when a cell was discovered in the *Batallón Blindado Bravos de Apure*, but the effect of the delation was more severe than expected, and attendance at the next congress of the movement, which was the fifth and last, was much lower than anticipated.

The five congresses were key in the shaping of the group's ideology, functioning dynamic, goals and organisation. Subjects such as the role the *FAN* should play in the revolutionary process were often on the table, with Chávez and his group claiming that it was the military who should drive the process, and others, among whom was Arias Cárdenas, considering that the armed forces should only agitate, and that the masses should be the ones to shape the transformation.

The group experienced intermittent periods of growth and shrinking, with the zenith being the period between the third congress, in 1985, and the discovery of the revolutionary officers in Apure the following year. Even at this point, however, one of the main failures of the *MBR-200* was that they had been unable to incorporate significant elements of other branches of the *FAN* into the conspiracy. Contacts in the Navy were basically non-existent, and the situation was not much better in the National Guard, where the sole significant contact was Captain Luis Felipe Acosta Carlez, Felipe Antonio's brother. In the Air Force, there had been a long-lasting friendship between Chávez and Luis Reyes Reyes, hailing both from Barinas, but no agreement had been made for a joint operation.

The relationship between the *MBR-200* and elements in the Air Force faced difficulties, as there were no significant conspiratorial groups headed by officers from the medium ranks that could be absorbed by them. Visconti's group was reduced and with a limited reach, and some hesitancy emanated from the fact that Visconti himself was about to gain a promotion to become a general, which would have had an impact on the functioning of the *MBR-200*'s leadership, which until then was mostly composed of majors and lieutenant colonels. Furthermore, one of the criticisms bestowed upon the *FAN* was that generals were, in the eyes of the conspirators, part of the political apparatus.

Multiple sources point at the civil disturbance of late February and early March 1989 as a turning point in the events that led to the rebellions of 1992. More specifically, the level of repression ordered by the government and the passivity showed by generals caused a break between them and the middle ranks. From that point onwards, the uprising became imminent, with various officers being contacted in units throughout the country, and politicians approached and offered posts in the government that would be established after the rebellion.

While the events of 1989 could be considered the catalyst, there were certainly other reasons cited by the rebels for their actions. The internal situation of the *FAN*, for example, where promotions were not granted on a meritorious basis, but rather on how well-connected officers were with members of either *Acción Democrática* or *Copei*, depending on which party was ruling the country. Corruption within the military also caused discontent among the conspirators, with various scandals tainting the institution's reputation. The one that immediately preceded the first uprising, in April 1990, was the Margold Case, which saw the disappearance of over 5 million dollars intended for the purchase of artillery ammunition from Spain. Furthermore, some of the interviewees for this work signalled the poor condition of both the military hardware

For days after the events of the *Caracazo* in February 1989, armoured cars of the Venezuelan Army could still be seen parked at the main road intersections in Caracas. (Albert Grandolini Collection)

A column of Dragoon 300 and Cadillac Gage V-100/150 Commando armoured car seen in the suburbs of Caracas in early March 1989. (Albert Grandolini Collection)

and the technical formation of certain groups of officers, which at the time was rushed because there was a shortage of qualified men to cover the number of vacancies for the lower officer ranks.[7] Both situations were associated to a generalised state of decay in some military units.[8]

DIM's Efforts: Too Little, Too Late

In late-November 1989, the *Dirección de Inteligencia Militar* (*DIM*, Directorate of Military Intelligence) intercepted communications between members of a conspiratorial group, which stated that an 'operation' was to be carried out on 3 December, coinciding with the first regional election ever held in Venezuela. The messages were signed with pseudonyms, with the apparent chief of the plan using the alias Zeus. Upon analysing the messages, it was concluded that Zeus was Chávez Frías,[9] and that, among the other officers that were identified, were Acosta Chirinos, Ortiz Contreras and Urdaneta Hernández. All of them were detained and interrogated, but rapidly liberated as several generals stated that those detained were 'good officers with deeply rooted democratic values.' This made Ochoa Antich believe that the conspiracy had its roots deeper within the *FAN*, with generals involved in the issue.

The possibility of the involvement of generals was further discussed when Chávez Frías and Urdaneta Hernández were assigned to new posts as commanders of the *Antonio Nicolás Briceño* and *Ramón García de Sena* paratrooper battalions, respectively, in mid-1990, although, in reality, the postings were merely circumstantial. This marked a new stage in the development of the conspiracy; one that was marked by tensions between the leadership and some of the young officers, and increased monitoring from the *DIM*.

Tension within the movement was mainly due to the execution of the operation, which the lower ranks wanted to carry out as soon as possible, through 1990 and 1991. This was primarily because of the pressure from the *DIM*, which interrogated some of them multiple times. The leadership, especially Chávez Frías, maintained that the uprising should not be rushed, and that the conditions were not ideal at the time.

During the third quarter of 1991, it was decided that the coup would take place on 10 December, which was Air Force Day. The *Antonio Nicolás Briceño* Battalion, commanded by Chávez Frías, was scheduled to perform a demonstration as part of a military parade which was to be attended by President Pérez and the military high command. Conspirators agreed that this was the most favourable scenario to carry out the operation. However, it was called off shortly before on Chávez's orders. He argued that it would not be safe to go ahead as some of the commanders of the *MBR-200* were not available, most notably Arias Cárdenas, who was studying in Israel, and Acosta Chirinos, who was in Brazil.

This situation almost led the *MBR-200* to collapse, as many of the young officers threatened to form a new conspiratorial group, and some even considered killing Chávez as he started to be seen as a traitor to the cause.[10] This lack of agreement regarding the day of the operation also caused some commanders to step back from it, including then-Major Raúl Isaías Baduel.

Despite this, the group still enjoyed good relations with political parties from the opposition, specially from the left. Alí Rodríguez Araque, Pablo Marcial Medina Carrasco, Kléber Ramírez Rojas, and the already-mentioned Douglas Bravo, all from the *Tercer* Camino, were in contact with the *MBR-200*, with some of them participating in meetings with the leaders of the movement. *La Causa R*, another leftist party, which enjoyed wide support in the southern state of Bolívar, was also in contact with the revolutionaries. In fact, the party's leader, Andrés Velásquez, who was also the governor of the aforementioned state, held talks with Chávez and other officers. They not only offered political support, but also people who would join the putschists when the uprising came.

With tensions still high within the movement, the news that the president would travel abroad came. He was to attend the annual meeting of the World Economic Forum, held in Davos, Switzerland, and was set to return late in the evening of 3 February. This, in conjunction with the internal crisis the group was going through, and the increasing pressure from the *DIM*, made the leadership pick this as the date of the uprising.

6

4 FEBRUARY 1992; EZEQUIEL ZAMORA OPERATIONS PLAN

The entirety of the details of the original plan for the uprising have never been made public. Before and after 1999, when Chávez Frías became president of Venezuela, the events of 1992 have been talked about in very biased terms. During the first period, it was shown as a senseless adventure by some politically ambitious officers, which aimed at overthrowing a democratic government and installing an authoritarian military regime its place. During the second one, the narrative changed, and it started to be considered a crusade of sorts in favour of Venezuela and its independence, which at the time were at the mercy of the United States of America and the local oligarchy. This is to say that while the political and ideological side has been widely studied and interpreted, the events, the plan itself, and even the casualties have been ignored, except when it is of interest for the interpreting party.

It is possible to assemble a picture of the original plan based on the part of it that was executed and knowing the cities where some of the units that were supposed to participate, but did not do so in the end, were garrisoned. However, differing versions obtained from documentary sources and interviews with those involved make it impossible at this time to formulate a hypothesis that could be considered as entirely loyal to the truth.

Two Theatres and Two Scenarios

It is certain that at least two theatres of operations were contemplated:

1. States of Lara, Mérida, Táchira, Trujillo and Zulia, whose commander was Francisco Arias Cárdenas, and
2. States of Aragua, Carabobo, Miranda and the Federal District of Caracas, commanded by Hugo Chávez.

It is possible that there was a third theatre, that likely included the states of Anzoátegui, Bolívar, Monagas and Sucre, which did not join the uprising when it got underway. The base for the latter assertion relies upon the claims of certain sources that the leaders of the uprising expected to receive support from elements from the 5ta *División de Infantería de Selva*.[1]

Modelled on the École *Militaire* in Paris, the Military Academy of Venezuela was constructed south of Caracas as three complexes, the centre of which is the huge Honour Courtyard. (Destacada)

Located in south-western Caracas, the Fuerte Tiuna or Fort Tiuna is a huge complex of military installations, including the Ministry of Defence, the General Command of the Army, the official residence of the vice president (Viñeta), and several units of the Venezuelan Military Academy. (Alba City)

Two scenarios were considered: the first one, in which Carlos Andrés Pérez was captured by the rebels in their first advance into Caracas, was seen as the ideal option as it implied a swift takeover of power. The second scenario contemplated the failure of the first attacks on the centres of political power, with the president managing to evade capture. This one would see the rebels falling back to Maracay to entrench themselves in the city while they waited for reinforcements from Arias Cárdenas' forces. In this case, the rebels were to cut off Caracas from the rest of the country by blockading all entrances to the city. Given that the rebel units from Aragua and Carabobo were the ones in charge of taking the city, this task was very likely assigned to units from the third theatre.

The *Antonio Nicolás Briceño*, *José Leonardo Chirinos* and *Ramón García de Sena* paratrooper battalions would spearhead the operation, commanded by Chávez Frías, Acosta Chirinos and Urdaneta Hernández, respectively. The latter would take Maracay, where all three were garrisoned, and secure the exit to Caracas for the armoured units of the *Batallón Blindado Pedro León Torres* that would join the rebellion from Valencia, while the first two would advance into the capital, with Chávez's battalion supporting the taking of the presidential palace, and Chirinos' covering multiple targets, including the Generalísimo Francisco de Miranda Airbase and the presidential residency. On the taking of Maracay, the *Ramón García de Sena* Battalion was to be assisted by the *Grupo de Artillería Bartolomé Salom*, commanded by Lieutenant Colonel David López Rivas; the *Judas Tadeo Piñango* Battalion, which was to be taken by Captain Pérez Sira; and elements from the *Batallón de Cazadores José Genaro Vásquez*, commanded by Ortiz Contreras. The latter unit was originally headquartered in Cumaná but had been deployed to Maracay days before to take a parachuting course.

Actions in Caracas were to be supported by local units, which included the *Caracas*, *Daniel Florencio O'Leary*, *Fernando Figueredo Mena*, *Francisco Carmona* and *Simón Bolívar* battalions; the *José Félix Ribas* Artillery Group; the *Juan Pablo Ayala* Cavalry Group; the *Agustín Codazzi* Engineering Regiment, composed of the *Tomás Farriar* and *Manuel Villapol* battalions; and the cadets of the Army Academy of the *AMV*. The five battalions were to participate in the taking of the presidential palace and residence, called Miraflores and La Casona, respectively, as well as other government dependencies and agencies like the El Helicoide complex, where the *Dirección de los Servicios de Inteligencia y Prevención* (*DISIP*, Directorate of Intelligence and Prevention Services) was headquartered. Other units were tasked with the taking of Fuerte Tiuna, the capital's main military complex, where the *AMV* and the Ministry of Defence are located, and assisting forces from Maracay and Valencia during their advance.

The other theatre had the mission of taking over the main cities of the west of the country, with Maracaibo being the command centre. As previously mentioned, the man in charge of the operation in the region was Lieutenant Colonel Francisco Javier Arias Cárdenas, commander of the *Grupo de Artillería Misilística José Gregorio Monagas*. José Rafael Angarita Gómez, commander of the *Grupo de Caballería Francisco Esteban Gómez*, was the second-in-command. One of the main obstacles Arias Cárdenas was to face lay within the walls of the same barracks where his unit was stationed. The *José Gregorio Monagas* Group shared the Libertador Barracks, located next to the abandoned Grano de Oro Airport, with the *Pedro María Freites* Group, whose commander, Lieutenant Colonel Rubén Darío Calderón Matheus, was not receptive when Arias Cárdenas tried to attract him to join the *MBR-200* months before.[2]

Located in Roca Tarpeya (San Pedro District of Caracas), the El Helicoide complex (seen here in the early 1960s, while still under construction) was originally meant to serve as a shopping centre. Instead, in 1984, it became the headquarters of the *DISIP* – and as such the centre of police investigations. With large parts converted into a detention centre, it also became the largest torture centre in Latin America. (Archivo Fotografia Urbana)

The construction of El Helicoide began in the late 1950s and was completed in 1961. Once a symbol of a rich and promising nation, by 1992, El Helicoide housed one of Venezuela's most infamous jails, and embodied the country's decline into a crisis zone. Unsurprisingly, it was heavily bombed by rebel-operated aircraft during the second coup attempt, when the dome was seriously damaged by unguided rockets and by anti-aircraft fire. (Archivo Fotografia Urbana)

The *José Gregorio Monagas* Group was, first, to take over Libertador Barracks, forcing the *Pedro María Freites* Group to participate in the uprising once its officers had been captured. Troops would then disperse through the city and the neighbouring town of Cabimas, taking control of key points such as La Chinita and Oro Negro airports; the local TV station, *Niños Cantores Televisión*; the General Rafael Urdaneta Bridge and the local government buildings, where officials would be apprehended, including the governor, Oswaldo Álvarez Paz.

The operation would be joined by men from the *Francisco Esteban Gómez* Group shortly after, as it was garrisoned in Fuerte Mara, a military complex in the northern outskirts of the city which they had to first take. By doing that, and after arresting their respective officers, other units from the *1era División de Infantería* would be

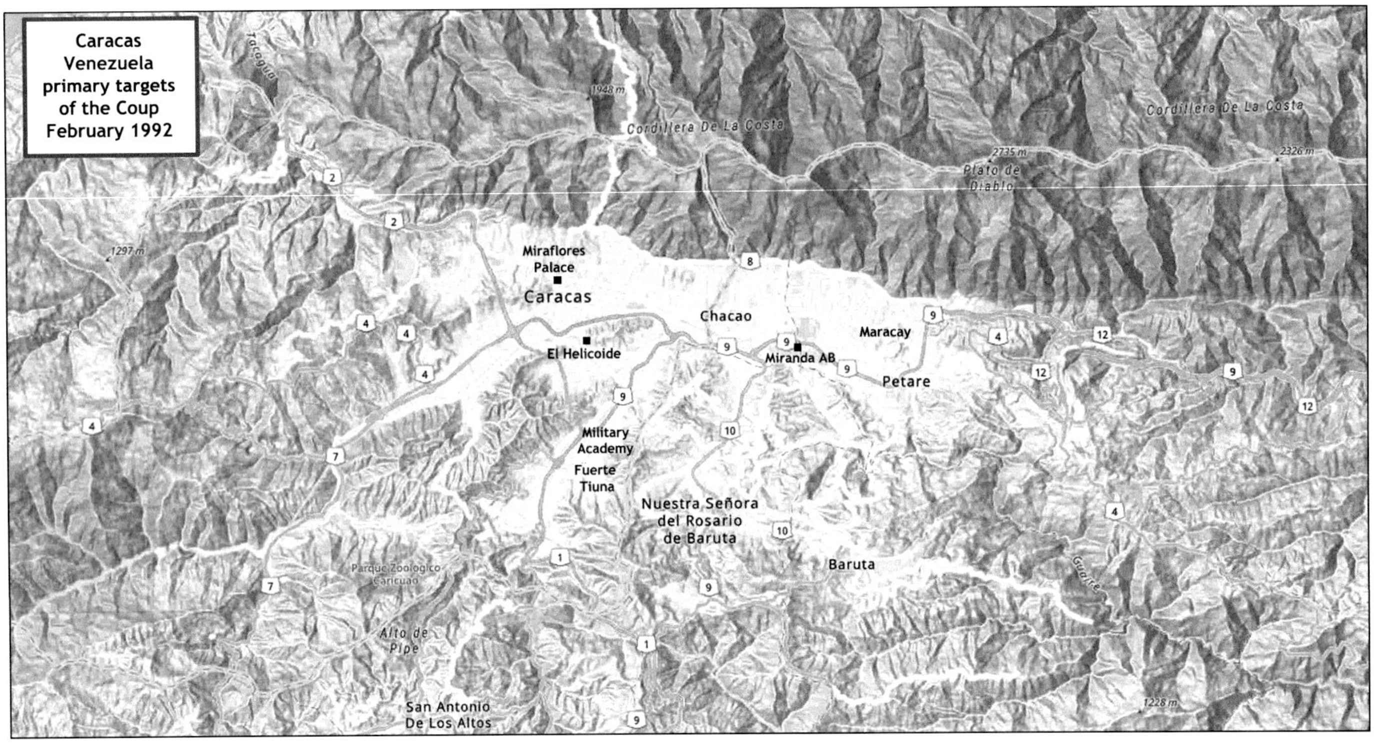

A map of Caracas with major objectives of the coup. (Map by Tom Cooper)

joining the uprising. Those included the *Bravos de Apure* Battalion, equipped with AMX-30 tanks; the *Francisco Aramendi* and *Carlos Soublette* mechanised and engineer battalions (respectively).

Once the main urban centres of the state of Zulia had been taken by rebels, they would then march east, towards Barquisimeto. There, they would remain on hold, waiting in case their assistance was required in Caracas. While they were there, they were to take the local military base, Fuerte Terepaima, located 15 kilometres south of the city.

Knowing the geographic area in which units from the third theatre would have acted, we can assert that it included not only elements of the *5ta División de Infantería de Selva*, garrisoned in Ciudad Bolívar, capital of the state of Bolívar, but also elements of the *3ra División de Infantería* garrisoned in El Tigre, Barcelona, Maturín and Cumaná, the latter three being the capitals of the states of Anzoátegui, Monagas and Sucre. The most likely scenario for them would have been a similar operation to that of the state of Zulia, taking key points in their respective cities and then marching to secondary locations to remain on hold to assist the operation in Caracas if the situation required so. However, as information on this third front is scarce, all we can do is speculate, which we will do no further than we already have.

The form of the government that would have resulted from the success of the rebellion is also a matter of controversy, as no official version exists, and different individual names and political parties and organisations have been mentioned through the years as members of what was to be a provisional government. As mentioned before, multiple members of leftist political entities were already involved in the movement. However, Captain Ismael Pérez Sira maintains that a multiple-member government had already been decided upon four years before the uprising. It was to be primarily civilian, but members from the military were to hold considerable influence. While he was not involved in the discussions with politicians, over 30 meetings of the *MBR-200*, the ones leading up to the uprising, were conducted in his house, which placed him at the epicentre of the negotiations. He asserts that the leadership of the resulting government *junta* would have most likely been held by either Kléber Ramírez Rojas or Carlos Tablante Hidalgo, then-governor of Aragua.[3]

The official version of the events does not mention what was to be the fate of President Pérez, had he been captured by the rebels. However, most sources suggest that killing him was never the goal, and that the most likely outcome for him was to face a public trial for the events of February 1989 and charges of embezzlement.

The rebels expected to enjoy significant support at street level from the population once they learned about the uprising. While this was not considered a key to the success of the operation, it was seen as an important boost for the legitimacy of the movement and the resulting government. The basis of this belief is the almost uninterrupted state of low-level rioting that had been ongoing through the country since early 1989.

The situation was such that the likelihood of a military uprising was commonly addressed in television and radio programs. It was openly stated that members of the officer ranks might be tempted to take advantage of the sentiment of discontent that was raging among the masses to intervene in politics through non-constitutional means. The traditional role that the *FAN* had played in the governance of the country was also considered by commenters. However, the appointment of Ochoa Antich as minister of defence in June 1991 somewhat dissipated these fears, as he was seen as a member of the military with deep constitutional values.

Preparations for the operation had started years before. According to Captain Pérez Sira, the possible targets of the operation were being discussed in late 1989. As soon as *MBR-200* members gained command, the recruitment of new personnel for the three airborne battalions prioritised the incorporation of natives of Caracas, who were familiar with the city's road system and layout.[4] Regarding this, it is important to note that, at the time, active conscription was the rule in Venezuela, with the mandatory military service lasting 24 months.

All three commanders commonly gave speeches to their troops, highlighting the situation of the country and asking rhetorical questions with clear political undertones. They also worked hard to form bonds with the troops, telling them as soon as they officially became part of their units that they were special and destined to achieve great things, but always in vague terms.[5]

In other cities, there had been unusual situations and attitudes by certain officers that, only after the rebellion occurred, came to be linked to the conspiracy. One of such cases was the insistence from the *Infantería de Marina* that it be designated in charge of the security of the Simón Bolívar International Airport; a role that had traditionally been in the hands of the National Guard.[6]

Miraflores Palace, the working office of the President of Venezuela, located on Urdaneta Avenue of central Caracas. (Prensa Presidencial)

7
A REBELLION IN TROUBLE

The consequences of the cancellation of the December 1991 operation were key in the eventual outcome of the 4 February uprising. The backing out of multiple officers left the operation without key units in various locations, with Caracas being the most important. Furthermore, the final operations plan had to be prepared hurriedly, with much of it being left to improvisation as the putsch unfolded. Adding to the pressure of the lower ranking officers to launch the coup, and the constant surveillance by the *DIM*, another reason to hurriedly execute the operation was that on 15 February, the *Antonio Nicolás Briceño* Battalion was to be deployed to the border with Colombia. Finally, rumours had been circulating for years that Chávez was the leader of a conspiratorial cell, but various circumstances had prevented in-depth investigations that could have uncovered the truth. However, Chávez and Ochoa Antich had a meeting in mid-January, in which the minister of defence warned Chávez that he would have no other option but to relieve him from the command of the battalion if rumours persisted.

Fateful Meeting

In late January 1992, Chávez and Reyes Reyes had a meeting. Reyes Reyes confided in Chávez that the situation in the Air Force was not optimal for it to join the uprising. Potential rebel sympathisers were few, scattered across the country, and not organised. At around the same date, Visconti was invited to one of the meetings in Pérez Sira's house, in which he exposed a similar situation, stating that all he could do was to delay the execution of any attack orders he received from his superiors as much as possible, something he described as 'active neutrality'.[1] As Chávez was not present in this meeting, an encounter between both was arranged by Reyes Reyes, which took place on 2 February.

The meeting took place in a restaurant outside Caracas in the afternoon. Visconti asked Chávez to delay the uprising by at least 90 days, so he could organise a faction within the Air Force that could provide air support to the rebels, to which Chávez responded explaining the vulnerable situation of the *MBR-200*. Once again, Visconti stated that all he could offer was his 'active neutrality'. At the time, Visconti was part of the commanding staff of El Libertador Airbase.

The decision to launch the coup on the night of 3 February was taken two days prior, when Lieutenant Colonel Arévalo Enrique Méndez Romero, a member of the Presidential Honour Guard who had graduated in the same class as Chávez, confirmed that President Pérez was going to arrive at Simón Bolívar International Airport on the evening of 3 February. The decision, however, was not communicated to most of the participating officers until the very day of the operation. Arias Cárdenas, for example, was informed shortly before midday, while Acosta Chirinos and Urdaneta Hernández were told early in the afternoon. Ortiz Contreras was the first to be informed, as he, as a guest officer in Maracay, spent most of the time with Chávez, who was the host. Through the morning of 3 February, several officers of the *Antonio Nicolás Briceño* Battalion were sent to Caracas to inform local sympathisers that the uprising was going to occur that night.

General Fernando Ochoa Antich, Minister of Defence of Venezuela as of February 1992. (El Nacional)

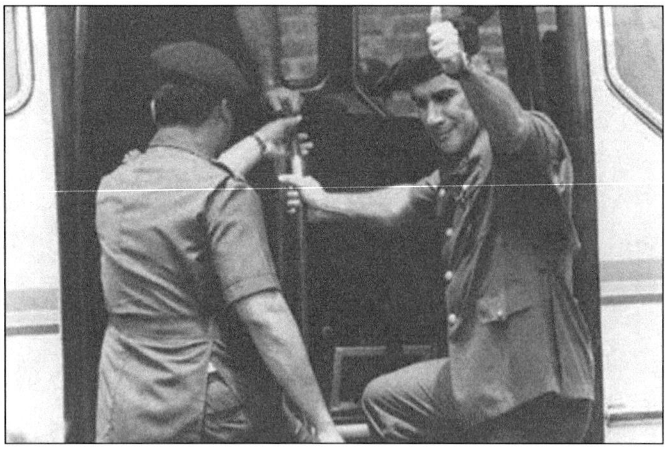

Urdaneta Hernández, one of three top coup plotters that was late in being informed about the decision to launch the attempt. (El Cooperante)

Roots of Failure

It was at that point in time that a series of issues that had been overlooked by the conspirators became evident: first, the number of *MBR-200* members that became disenchanted after the fiasco of December 1991 was underestimated. When the messengers in question contacted officers in the *Daniel Florencio O'Leary* and *Simón Bolívar* battalions, some of the responses they received were negative. They got similar responses when they went to meet local leaders of the political parties that had promised forces to support the operation, citing the fact that they had had little time to prepare as the reason. On top of that, most of the rebel officers that were stationed in Caracas at the time held no command positions, with most of them being either staff of the *AMV* or holding administrative jobs. However, these were not the only significant issues the rebellion would suffer from.

Captain René Alejandro Gimón Álvarez was one of the few officers in Caracas that had been informed of the date of the operation on 1 February, having been told by captains Ronald José Blanco La Cruz and Antonio Rafael Rojas Suárez, who were also among the aforementioned messengers the next day. Being part of the staff of the *AMV*, he was tasked with igniting the insurrection there, along with other members of the conspiracy. They were to arm the cadets of the last two courses, take over the compound and take most of them as reinforcements to the places that were going to be assaulted by the main forces.

In the process of taking control of the *AMV*, Gimón Álvarez was supposed to take the director of the institution, General Manuel Delgado Gainza, prisoner. This specific task, by itself, was easy to comply with. However, on a personal level for Gimón Álvarez, it was not as simple as it seemed to be, as he had been dating Delgado Gainza's daughter for around one month. After evaluating the tough situation he was in, Gimón Álvarez went to Delgado Gainza's office shortly before 11:00, telling him about the coup d'état attempt that was to take place that night.

Delgado requested an urgent appointment with General Pedro Remigio Rangel Rojas, general commander of the Army, which took place shortly after midday. According to Ochoa Antich, Rangel wanted to talk directly with Gimón Álvarez before taking further action. While he waited for the captain to arrive, Delgado informed General Reinaldo Valero Rivas, chief of the intelligence service of the Army, who ordered that a letter warning of a possible uprising be prepared for all units.

Gimón Álvarez arrived at around 14:30, and his meeting with Rangel Rojas took place at 15:00. After this meeting was finished, Rangel summoned Valero Rivas, who informed him of what he had been told by Delgado a few hours earlier. Rangel's reaction was dismissive, stating that the information was old and based on unfounded rumours. Consequently, he also rejected sending the warning letter that had been redacted on Valero's orders earlier. He, however, ordered the setting-up of pre-emptive checkpoints on the road network of Fuerte Tiuna, the deployment of extra forces around the General Command of the Army, and a review of the status of all units of the *1ra División de Infantería*, of which the *Caracas* and *Daniel Florencio O'Leary* battalions were part. Despite this, the fact that he did not issue a generalised warning, and that ordered the rumours to be investigated, are considered by Ochoa Antich as a clear sign that he did not believe there was an actual risk of an uprising that day. This, on top of the fact that Ochoa himself was not warned at any point by any of the generals involved in the meetings.

At around 18:00, Rojas Suárez was warned by a source within the *DIM* that the government had knowledge of the plan. An hour later, he met with Blanco La Cruz; Gerardo Alfredo Márquez Reina, who was another rebel captain; and a group of officers from the *AMV* who were also involved with the *MBR-200*, to evaluate the situation. They naturally concluded that the plan had little chances of success, but that, at that point, it was impossible to stop it from being executed, and that their involvement would be eventually discovered even if they did not join the operation. The final decision was to carry on.

When this meeting came to an end, at around 19:00, the situation in Caracas was dire. The *MBR-200* officers in the *Caracas*, *Daniel Florencio O'Leary*, *Simón Bolívar*, *Fernando Figueredo Mena* and *Francisco Carmona* battalions had communicated that they would not join the rebellion, and only the small *José Félix Ribas* and *Juan Pablo Ayala* groups of artillery and cavalry, respectively, had confirmed their participation.

It was not until after 20:00 that Ochoa Antich was informed of the rumours that had been circulating the entire day. He had been in Maracaibo the whole day, coordinating a vaccination plan that was to involve military doctors in remote indigenous communities. Upon returning to Caracas, he was informed that General Freddys Ventura Maya Cardona, commander of the National Guard, needed to have an urgent conversation with him. It was through that phone call that the minister of defence learned of the situation. Before making it to Caracas, he ordered his driver to head back to Maiquetía Airport, where he had landed less than an hour prior. He changed his mind before getting there and ordered the driver to go to the local National Guard detachment, number 53, instead, which at the time was commanded by Lieutenant Colonel Marco Ferreira Torres. This unit oversaw providing security to the airport.

Ferreira had been alerted of the rumours earlier that day. Knowing that the president was to land at 22:00, approximately, he expected the usual security device to be deployed two hours before. However, by 21:00 it had not arrived. Furthermore, at around 20:30, he received a call from Maya Cardona ordering him not to abandon the detachment and telling him that a member of the *DIM* was on the way to deliver confidential information to him. The officer in question never arrived, but he received a request from a lower ranking member of the *DIM* that was stationed at the airport that six FALs be lent to them, to which Ferreira refused, as he considered suspicious that the request did not come directly from the local officer in charge.[2]

Ferreira considered the situation was suspicious enough and ordered his men to take over the airport and its surroundings.[3] When Ochoa Antich made it to the detachment, at around 21:30, he found the area to be entirely militarised. He then sent a messenger, Sublieutenant Sabino José Vigil Rodríguez, to alert the *Infantería de Marina* of the situation. Almost at the same time, the security detail for the arrival of the president, composed of members of the Presidential Honour Guard and of civilian agencies, like *DISIP* and the *Policía Técnica Judicial* (*PTJ*), hurriedly prepared.

The president landed shortly after 22:00, being surprised by the presence of Ochoa Antich at the airport. When he was told about the rumours that had been circulating all day, he was visibly bothered and dismissive, but nevertheless told the minister to be at his office early in the morning of the next day to start an investigation. Less than an hour later, the presidential motorcade arrived in La Casona, the official residence of the President of the Republic.

The Plan Gets Underway

The first troop movement was made even before the plot was discovered. At 09:00, a section of 20 men under command of Major Francisco Javier Centeno and Lieutenant Freddy Rodríguez González was dispatched from the *Antonio Nicolás Briceño* Battalion towards the Campo de Carabobo, southeast of Valencia. There, they would join the *24 de junio* Company, which was an organic part of the Presidential Honour Guard, and remain on hold for the actions that would take place later that day. The *24 de junio* Company was commanded by Captain Ángel Orlando Martínez Alfonzo and performed ceremonial tasks at the site of the Battle of Carabobo. At 17:00, reinforcements were sent from Maracay: approximately 150 soldiers from both the *Antonio Nicolás Briceño* and *José Genaro Vásquez* battalions.

In Maracay, the rebellion started at a number of different spots between 20:30 and 21:00. The takeover of the Páez Barracks, as well as that of the La Placera military complex, were swift. It was there where the *José Leonardo Chirinos*, *Antonio Nicolás Briceño* and *Ramón García de Sena* battalions were garrisoned, respectively. The remaining elements of the *José Genaro Vásquez* Battalion were also in the Páez Barracks.

In that half-hour period, soldiers were hurriedly ordered to form-up in the respective yards. They all noted the presence of multiple public transport units at the premises, which had been procured since the previous day by the rebel officers. For that, they had the perfect cover: the *José Leonardo Chirinos* and *Antonio Nicolás Briceño* battalions were scheduled to take part in training manoeuvres the following day in El Pao, in the state of Cojedes. That cover was also used earlier in the day for the issuance of war material to the troops, who were told they would depart before sunrise the following day.

A still from a video showing rebel troops moving along the wall of the presidential palace. (UN)

> We were issued full gear, including empty magazines, at around 15:00, which was not uncommon given that we were supposed to participate in maneuvers the following day. The first strange thing we noticed was that, around three hours later, we were ordered to go to the armoury to pick up more equipment, which we found out were live rounds, grenades, rocket launchers and other pieces of equipment we never used in exercises; we were always issued blanks, and it was done when we got to the training grounds, not while we were still in Maracay.[4]

When the rebellion started, most commanding officers that were not part of the *MBR-200* were not in the garrisons, as normal activities for the day had already been finished. The few that remained, mostly captains and majors, were offered two options: join the rebellion or be detained in the barracks until the operation was over. This task was executed almost exclusively by rebel officers, as they wanted to keep the troops oblivious as to what was going to happen.

Urdaneta Hernández's men captured the command building of the *42da Brigada de Infantería Paracaidista*, of which the three main rebel battalions were part. The commander of the brigade, General Carlos Moreno Guarache, was not there, but he talked over the phone with Urdaneta, who explained to him what was happening, told him that any effort to stop the rebellion was going to be futile, and suggested that he stay at home and avoid being detained by the rebels. Moreno Guarache obeyed and did not interfere with what his unit was doing.

Maracay

The plan for the taking of Maracay contemplated that the *Ramón García de Sena* and *José Genaro Vásquez* battalions would take the eastern part of the city, while the *Bartolomé Salom* Artillery Group would take the west. The objectives for the forces operating in the first sector included El Libertador Airbase and the administrative facilities of the *4ta División de Infantería*, as well as the roads heading to Caracas. In the second sector, López Rivas' forces were to detain the governor of Carabobo, Henrique Salas Römer; capture Mariscal Sucre Airbase; and the Mérida Barracks, where the *Batallón de Armamento Manuel Toro* was garrisoned.

> Being part of the *Ramón García de Sena* Battalion, I was part of the group that took El Libertador Airbase. Shortly before 22:00, we were already being distributed through the city. Before getting to our designated point, I asked a lieutenant, with whom I consider I was relatively close, what was going on. He told me that there was a coup d'état underway, and that we were going to support the government.[5]

However, the plan was to face yet another major setback merely hours before starting: a part of López Rivas' unit was performing exercises in the state of Cojedes. The commander had stated that he would reunite his troops at mid-afternoon in Maracay. He departed Maracay at 15:00, approximately, and did not come back. Considering that it was of vital importance for the uprising to establish control over the city, the goals remained the same and had to be achieved with fewer troops than initially expected.

Valencia

The uprising in Valencia was similarly swift. The *MBR-200* officer in charge of taking the city was Captain Luis Rafael Valderrama Rosales. At the time of the uprising, he was not in a command position, as he was a student officer at the *Instituto Universitario*

The first armoured cars rolling down the streets of Caracas, near the Presidential Palace, late on 3 February 1992. (UN)

Politécnico de las Fuerzas Armadas (*IUPFAN*, Polytechnic University Institute of the National Armed Forces). However, until two years before, he had served in the *Grupo de Artillería Autopropulsada Jacinto Lara*, which was part of the *41^{era} Brigada Blindada*, stationed in Fuerte Paramacay. The *Pedro León Torres* Battalion belonged to this unit as well. There were other rebel officers still serving in the brigade, including captains Darío Noel Arteaga Páez, Wilmer Omar Barrientos Fernández, Ángel Godoy Chávez and Pedro José Jiménez Yusti. They had been informed that the operation would take place that day shortly after midday.

> The only uncommon things we noticed preceding the uprising was that the amount of work that was being done in our base was, on one hand, more than usual; but in the other one, less. What I'm trying to say is that, while we were ordered to check the operational status of every single tank in the unit and to perform unscheduled maintenance if required, we were also allowed to wake up a couple of hours later than usual, our exercises would be lighter, and food rations were larger. At the time, while we noticed that such things were uncommon, we suspected nothing. Soldiers just enjoyed the situation. Also, on the day of the uprising, officers were nowhere to be seen during the day.[6]

By 19:00, the commanders of the *Jacinto Lara* and *José Gabriel Lugo* groups had left Fuerte Paramacay. Also absent was the commander of the brigade, Lieutenant Colonel Luis Carlos Bermúdez Alarcón, who had been on leave for three days at the time of the uprising. Theoretically, in this situation, few were the obstacles Valderrama Rosales would face when taking the base. It was shortly after that time that troop movements started.

> At around 20:30, all platoon commanders were summoned by Sergeant Andrés Rangel Acosta, who ordered us, section leaders, to get our men and vehicles fully geared up. The garrison immediately came back to life after a dull day. You could hear orders being shouted; the running engines of the Scorpion 90 tanks, of which we had 33; the typical metal-on-metal sound of ammo belts being moved… I loaded up my tank with AT rounds and ensured my men had all their gear in order. At this point we knew something was going on, we just weren't sure of what it was. We'd never been ordered to gear-up so suddenly outside regular drills, and even then, we were never issued live ammunition, both for soldiers and the vehicles. Past 21:30, the officers showed up, we were summoned once again and were explicitly told what was going to happen that night. Those who didn't want to participate were told they would be detained in the cells of the base until the rebellion was over, without any further consequences. However, all of us agreed to take part.[7]

It took around two hours to secure the city, which was firmly under rebel control before 01:00. Twenty tanks under command of Captain Godoy Chávez departed east, they were to support the operations in Caracas, passing through the already-taken Maracay on their way there, and transferring four tanks to the *Ramón García de Sena* Battalion. The remaining ones participated in the takeover of Valencia, which included taking, among other positions, the Arturo Michelena International Airport, the headquarters of the Carabobo State Police, and the regional command of the National Guard. Paradoxically, the only major position that the rebels were unable to fully control was Fuerte Paramacay itself, as things did not go as expected when not all units agreed to participate in the uprising. A part of the base was taken by the rebels, while the other one remained under loyalist control. There was no exchange of fire in the facility, however.

Among the minor objectives in the city that we mentioned before were local radio stations, all secured without resistance. Calls for the population to gather in front of Fuerte Paramacay were made, and a crowd of civilians started blocking the accesses of the facility within an hour. During the opening stage of the rebellion, this prevented loyalist units from going into the city to fight the rebels. Surrounding was also the tactic used to neutralise the National Guard forces stationed in the local regional command. Approximately at 23:00, the facility was surrounded by an infantry company and 12 tanks of the *Pedro León Torres* Battalion, as well as an unspecified number of AMX-13s of the *Jacinto Lara* Group under command of Barrientos Fernández.

Some of the rebel forces deployed to the city had orders to detain loyalist officers in their houses, which was the case of Colonel Henry Rangel Fuentes, Chief of Staff of the Brigade. As he was leaving his house after learning of the rebellion, he was intercepted by Arteaga Páez and his men and taken to the rebel-controlled part of Fuerte Paramacay, where other officers who refused to join the rebellion were also being held. All of them were offered the possibility of joining the uprising, with the majority refusing to do so.

Another participant, from a different unit, offers a different perspective of the events in Valencia:

> At the time I was about to finish my mandatory military service and was merely one month away from being discharged. Around eight months before, I had been selected to be part of the serving staff of the officer's mess, so I was not usually with regular troops through the day. After the dinner service had been finished, I headed to my bunk, only to be ordered to go to the yard by a lieutenant a few minutes later. When I got there, there was a lot of activity going on, with one officer explaining [to] a group of soldiers that we were going to be sent to deal with riots at the local university. I only started to suspect the reason of our mobilisation was something else when, first of all, soldiers were taking weapons out of the armoury without any kind of control, while being told to do it faster by the officer in charge, who was usually a very methodical man when it came to issuing war material; and second, when I was given not only a FAL, but also live rounds and rifle grenades, while other soldiers were carrying AFAGs, and AT4s, and scoped M14s. That is, quite clearly, not anti-riot gear. Still not being sure of what was going on, we were ordered to board some trucks that were already there when I first got to the yard and started to be distributed through the city. It

was then that I saw some officers with uniforms of the airborne brigade, which I thought was odd. As soon as we left the base, we turned not towards the university, but towards the opposite direction. That's when the possibility of it being a coup d'état first crossed my mind, but I was still thinking we were going to fight the rebels, not that we were the mutineers.[8]

San Juan de los Morros

Southeast of Maracay is San Juan de los Morros, capital of the state of Guárico. Stationed at the local military facility, Fuerte Conopoima, was the *Batallón Misilístico Antitanque Ezequiel Zamora*, equipped with Israeli-made MAPATS ATGM systems, and commanded by Lieutenant Colonel Efraín Enrique Flores Tejera. Also headquartered there was the *Grupo de Caballería Ambrosio Plaza*. On the day of the uprising, Flores Tejera and part of his staff were on duty in Caracas, and the provisional commander of the battalion was Captain Edgar Antonio Hernández Behrens, a member of the *MBR-200*. He had been informed by Lieutenant Jesús Rafael Suárez Chourio – one of the messengers sent by Chávez to different units – at around 13:00 on 3 February that the uprising would take place that day.

As he was the officer in charge of the unit, Hernández Behrens did not face many obstacles to the preparation of his men. The initial task of the *Ezequiel Zamora* Battalion consisted of supporting the advance from Maracay to Caracas, and taking the town of Charallave, south of the capital, and to resist any loyalist advance from that direction. By 14:00 all rebel officers from the unit had been informed, and preparations were underway. Before the insurrection started, approximately at 22:00, Hernández Behrens received a call from Blanco La Cruz to inform him that, instead of occupying Charallave, his men should push into Caracas and support the taking of Fuerte Tiuna.

Flores Tejera was not expected to arrive until mid-morning of the following day. However, he returned to San Juan de los Morros at 23:00, when local units had not yet rebelled. He asked Hernández Behrens to brief him on the activities performed through the day, which delayed the mobilisation of the rebel forces. Their meeting lasted until approximately 23:30, after which Flores Tejera went to sleep. Immediately, Hernández Behrens dispatched his forces to the points they had been assigned. The 12 Scorpion 90s of the *Ambrosio Plaza* Group marched towards Maracay.

Maracaibo

In Maracaibo, Arias Cárdenas and Angarita Gómez relied on surprise for the success of the opening hours of the operation. They had been unable to convince a significant number of officers to join the *MBR-200*, with only four captains and two lieutenants being compromised with the rebellion. At 09:30, Arias Cárdenas called Angarita Gómez to check upon the preparations for the takeover of Fuerte Mara. However, he was told that local units would not be joining the rebellion, as the chances of success were considered slim.

Without Angarita Gómez's forces taking over the military base, loyalist units could now march into Maracaibo and dispute control of the city with Arias Cárdenas' men, who were inferior both in firepower and number. However, the rebellion could not be aborted, and Arias Cárdenas decided to proceed. He decided to keep Angarita's decision secret and spent most of the day driving through the city with captains José Albarrán Barrios and Moisés González López, and Lieutenant Gustavo Torrealba Machado, showing them the points of the city they would have to take that night. They returned to Libertador Barracks after 17:00 to start preparing the troops for the operation. At 22:30, he was the only commander in the barracks. He called for an urgent meeting with all officers from his group, in which he explained what was going to happen and invited them to join, which all agreed to do. This way, both the *José Gregorio Monagas* and *Pedro María Freites* groups were under Arias Cárdenas' control.

Through the day, I did not notice anything uncommon. Shortly before 23:00, I was woken up by a lieutenant and told to gear-up and go to the yard, to which I protested, because I, being the personal driver of Calderón Matheus, was usually exempt from unscheduled drills. He reaffirmed the order and said it was not a drill. Grudgingly, I went to the yard and found people running in different directions, carrying crates of ammunition and full combat gear, and a column of M35 trucks ready to depart to the city. I was then told to go with a group of soldiers to pick up our gear in one of the armouries, which happened to be the only one among the four in Libertador Barracks whose officer in charge, Lieutenant Germán Darío Áñez Olivares, refused to hand [over]. I witnessed as he threw the keys over the roof, and then as he surrendered himself to Arias Cárdenas, after which he was escorted into the dungeons underneath the facilities. Arias tried to open the door by shooting at it with his handgun, to no avail; he had to borrow a FAL from another soldier to break the lock. I entered the armoury last, taking the last two rifles left, one of which I went to leave in my closet. As I was going back to the yard, I noticed the door of Calderón Matheus' office was open, so I went to check. There, I found a group of officers of the *José Gregorio Monagas* Group destroying all communications equipment and going through my commander's belongings. They, being of a higher rank than me, ordered me to leave. I went to Arias Cárdenas once again and asked him what his men were doing in Calderón Matheus' office. He told me not to worry, that my commander was aware of what was going on and that he was on his way to the barracks, and that there was something strange going on in the country, without giving further details. After some minutes, he addressed a group of soldiers saying that there was a coup d'état going on and that we were going to fight against the putschists. But, immediately after, he went to complain about the situation of the country, which left us all confused. After that, we were distributed under command of different rebel officers and loaded into the M35s, on which we took Maracaibo. I was sent to the local *DISIP* headquarters on El Milagro Avenue, and was under command of a lieutenant I was not familiar with, and whose name I can't recall. All I know is that he was from Arias Cárdenas' unit.[9]

Caracas

Finally, the uprising in Caracas was minor in scale, as the size and number of units involved was the smallest. Furthermore, their area of activity was limited to Fuerte Tiuna, where they would secure the roads to clear the passage of other rebel units and capture key buildings, including the General Command of the Army, the *AMV* and other administrative dependencies of the *FAN*. They would also try to take over other units and force them to join the rebellion.

After taking Fuerte Tiuna and securing the highway that passes next to it, they would remain on hold until units from Maracay and San Juan de los Morros arrived. They would then join the paratroopers and assist them in the taking of other key points in Caracas.

Shortly before 22:00, majors Pedro Emilio Alastre López and Carlos Díaz Reyes; and captains Blanco La Cruz, Rojas Suárez, Noel

Rafael Martínez Rivero and Carlos Luis Aguilera Borjas entered the facility where the *Juan Pablo Ayala* and *José Félix Ribas* groups were garrisoned and promptly imprisoned the commanders, lieutenant colonels Luis Contreras Acevedo and Carlos Rodríguez Barrios, respectively. This was facilitated by Captain Joaquín Napoleón Suárez Montes, lieutenants Joaquín Alberto González Dorta and Florencio Antonio Porras Echezuría; and Sublieutenant Gerardo Goyo Regardiz, who were members of the *MBR-200*.

Soldiers of both units were ordered to form-up in the yard and given a speech by Rojas Suárez, in which he explained that a coup d'état was taking place, and that they were going to fight rebel units, which had already taken control of part of the facilities in Fuerte Tiuna. He also stated that reinforcements would come from Maracay, Valencia and other garrisons, which included paratroopers and armoured units.

Also within the premises of Fuerte Tiuna, the *Agustín Codazzi* Regiment was simultaneously being taken over by other rebel officers, namely: captains Humberto Ortega Díaz, Edgar Antonio Graterol Santos and Jesús Alberto Aguilarte Gámez; lieutenants Rafael Gerardo Oldenburg Arráiz and Winston Eduardo Gámez Vizcaya; and Sublieutenant Eloy Arzola Cedeño. With the natural officers not being present, the rebels faced no resistance in the taking of the unit. They rapidly announced the reason of their presence there, stating the same purpose as the other rebel officers in Fuerte Tiuna. Immediately, a mixed company composed by men of the two battalions of the regiment, led by Aguilarte Gámez, went on foot to take the Ministry of Defence, located less than two kilometres away from the garrison.

> We, as soldiers, had not even heard about the rumours of an uprising. We only came to know about it when we returned to our garrison, at around 22:15, after attending nocturnal high school classes. Upon arriving, we found our fellow soldiers in formation while some officers were delivering a speech. Immediately after, we were ordered to go to the armoury, issued full combat gear and loaded into M35 trucks. As we drove through the internal roads of Fuerte Tiuna, several units broke off the formation, heading to their designated spots. Ours was the General Command of the Army building, and we were under command of two young sublieutenants that we had never seen before; De Freitas and Toro, were their surnames. We were told to use surprise to overpower the sentinels in front of the building, which worked out. Then, we took a part of the premises without facing resistance until we came across a part of the defending forces that had entrenched themselves in the upper floors of the building. The many prisoners we took, which included officers that were spending the night in the dormitories of the facility, were placed in the conference room, while awaiting further instructions from Porras Echezuría and González Dorta, who oversaw the operations in which I participated.[10]

One of the reasons why these units in Fuerte Tiuna were taken without difficulties by rebel officers was because, for unknown reasons, the warning message issued earlier in the day by General Rangel Rojas' office was not delivered to their commanders.

Operations in Maracay, San Juan de los Morros and Valencia

Given the relative ease with which the rebels captured both Maracay and Valencia, there were no major engagements there. It is accurate to say that, except for the failure to take the entirety of Fuerte Paramacay and El Libertador Airbase, the operations in both cities were a success, as the main goal, which was to clear the way for the tanks that were to go to Caracas, was achieved.

In Maracay, there were skirmishes and engagements with forces from both the Air Force and the National Guard that lasted for hours and left casualties. Most of them were against the second branch, as there were checkpoints all along the route the spearhead rebel forces had to secure. However, the most significant took place in El Libertador Airbase, south of the city.

The airfield was of vital importance for the rebels, as capturing it would deprive loyalists of a good part of their aerial assets. However, for reasons that to this day remain a source of dispute, the base was not entirely occupied by the putschists, who limited their advance to the residences of officers and certain administrative buildings. According to General Ochoa Antich, on the afternoon of 3 February, Chávez told Urdaneta Hernández that General Visconti had decided to join them, and that the *Ramón García de Sena* Battalion would only have to surround the base and not allow anyone to enter, to which Urdaneta Hernández agreed, as this would allow him to use more troops in other parts of the city. However, this account remains disputed, as a different version of the events states that the *FAV* forced the rebels not to take the whole base with threats of bombing them.

The officers in charge of taking the facility were Major Carlos Luis Torres Numberg and Lieutenant Juan Carlos DuBoulay Perozo. They would be reinforced by four Scorpion 90 tanks from the *Pedro León Torres* Battalion, which arrived after the unit started deploying in the surrounding areas of the base, at approximately 22:15.

> We entered the perimeter of the base facing basically no resistance, as the sentinels in the entrance laid down their weapons as soon as they realised they were outnumbered and outpowered by us. During the first hour, I was part of the group that was guarding the main entrance to the facility, and our orders were not to allow anyone, civilian or military, to enter or exit the base. Shortly before 23:00, many officers started to arrive, mostly from the Air Force, pilots, and all. We would disarm them and turn them back, without taking them prisoners because that was not part of our orders. To give you an idea, we managed to fill to the brim two ALICE backpacks with handguns and magazines that we took from the officers in question. At around 23:15, our officers decided that we'd push further into the perimeter of the base, and I was one of those sent deeper into the facility. When we reached the officer residences, the place was desolate; all lights in the buildings were off, and just a few of the sidewalk lights were

A Dragoon 300VZ armoured car deployed outside Miraflores Palace, late on 3 February 1992. (Albert Grandolini Collection)

A Cadillac Gage V-100 Commando armoured car in the backyard of Miraflores. (Albert Grandolini Collection)

> working. We even thought we had advanced into an abandoned part of the base; we had never been there, we were unfamiliar with the place. We, however, kept advancing. After a few dozen meters we realised that we were being pointed at by members of the *Policía Aérea* from rooftops and watch towers. When they realised that we had already noticed their presence, one of them started shooting and killed one of our comrades. We returned fire, and they fell back; but I don't think we hit anyone. We did not advance any further and maintained that position for the rest of the night.[11]

The commander of the airbase, General Juan Antonio Paredes Niño, had been detained in the opening hours of the rebellion and taken to the Páez Barracks, as rebel leaders considered neutralising him a key factor for their success. In this situation, the next in the chain of command was General Visconti Osorio, who assumed the function of commander as soon as he learned of Paredes Niño's detention. To ensure his position, he summoned all commanders present in the base and explained the ongoing situation, stating that, to prevent a takeover of the facility, he would try to keep it neutral.

When Torres Numberg's troops were already deployed around the base, Visconti sent Reyes Reyes to meet him. This is where the dispute we mentioned becomes relevant again, as a differing version of the event states that, during this meeting, which took place approximately at 23:00, Torres Numberg specified that he had orders to take the entirety of the base and asked Reyes to order the *Policía Aérea* to lay down their weapons. Reyes answered that he was not in charge and that he would talk with his superior. He informed Visconti, who decided to personally meet Torres. It was between the two meetings that the rebels advanced deeper into the facility. During their conversation, Torres made clear that he would not give up on taking the base, to which Visconti replied that, if his men kept advancing, he would have them attacked from the air. To make the threat more credible, he ordered two F-16s to take-off and fly low over their positions. It was only then that Torres agreed to maintain his current ground.

This version offers a different scenario to the one we described before, and there are no reliable sources that favour one version or the other. The fact is, however, that the rebels did not establish total control over El Libertador Airbase, which was a key factor in the failure of their operation.

The second airbase in Maracay, Mariscal Sucre, where the *EAM* is located, was taken without resistance by lieutenants Raffaele Giovanni Lepore Ferrante, Félix Ramón Osorio Guzmán and Luis Taboada González, with its officers being taken prisoners and locked in the underground dungeons of the Páez Barracks. The officers from the 21st Detachment of the National Guard, located in the southern part of the city, which was also taken facing minimal resistance, had the same treatment.

Minor engagements occurred on the taking of the National Guard checkpoints located in the entrances and exits of the city, most importantly in the *La Cabrera* tunnel, which links the city to Valencia, and La Encrucijada, a major intersection at the eastern end of the urban centre, on the way to Caracas. After both points were taken, the first was left in charge of Lieutenant José Chávez Mayora, while Pérez Sira stayed in the second.

> The checkpoint at the La Cabrera tunnel is bigger than the average. As it was the middle of the night, we easily overpowered the two sentinels outside, and then proceeded to storm the dormitories. As soon as we entered, and I was the first in the line, a lieutenant retrieved an Uzi from under his mattress and shot in my direction, but no one was hit. I managed to disarm him, after which he started crying and saying he was sorry. Something similar happened when we went to take La Encrucijada. When we arrived, those who were inside heard us, and as soon as we

> entered, once again I was first in the line, the first thing I saw was the barrel of a FAL pointing at me. After a shouting match, the National Guard was convinced by his comrades to surrender, as they were all being pointed at by my men.[12]

At the other end of the tunnel, in Valencia, besides the tense situation inside of the now-divided Fuerte Paramacay, the only significant engagement was that at Arturo Michelena International Airport, whose two detachments of the National Guard resisted the rebel advance.

> When we got to the airport, we didn't go to the main terminal, as there was another group going to take care of that; we went to the piloting school of the National Guard, where helicopter crews are formed. It is a small building in the western end of the airport perimeter, which many years ago was the passenger terminal. Immediately, our officer in command, a lieutenant that I hadn't seen before, and whose surname was Hernández, got off the truck and directly, megaphone-in-hand, yelled: "Gentlemen of the National Guard, this is a coup d'état. Surrender yourselves and nothing bad will happen to you!". Only then we realised that it was us who were trying to oust the government. It all happened so fast, that by the time he finished talking, most of us were still aboard the trucks. The response of the guards was equally fast, as they immediately started shooting. As the exchange of fire was raging, some of us managed to go around the building and surprise them from behind, and they immediately surrendered, ending the engagement after 20 minutes. We took all 26 of them prisoners, but we let them go after disarming them and having them wear civilian clothing. This was a mistake; they returned around half an hour later, now with reinforcements, to recapture the building. However, we managed to resist, and they retired again. Considering the intensity of the shootouts, I can only consider a miracle the fact that there were no deaths on either side. Surprisingly, a pair of these guards returned shortly after and asked to join us in the rebellion. We took them in, and they showed us which places we should reinforce, shall more loyalist forces come.[13]

The taking of the main terminal building was not met with as much resistance, as the group in charge had a tank supporting them.

> As soon as we got there, our officer in command, a lieutenant from one of the paratrooper battalions headquartered in Maracay, told the National Guard captain that was the officer in charge that he had orders to take control of the airport because there was a possible coup d'état going on, and that we had to protect it in case rebels came to take it. The captain replied that he had not been informed of such a thing, and asked the lieutenant to wait with his men outside of the building while he asked his superior about the situation, to which our commander agreed. It was a very cordial conversation. We went to the parking [area], right in front of the building, where our tank, a Scorpion 90, was. The lieutenant ordered the gunner to strafe the terminal building with two entire boxes of ammunition using the coaxial gun. That must have been 400 or 450 rounds. Immediately after, with our ears still ringing, he yelled through a megaphone: "The rebels have arrived. You have 15 seconds to hand yourselves [over], or else we'll assault the terminal and take no prisoners!". Immediately, the guards started coming out one by one with their hands up. There were around 15 of them, whom we tied and locked in a storage room. An element of five men was left guarding the terminal building, while the rest of us went to set up a checkpoint at the beginning of the road that heads to the airport, about one kilometre away. Through the night, we had sporadic engagements with the State Police and the *DISIP*, who at times positioned themselves at the next intersection, some 500 meters away, and exchanged fire with us, without causing casualties on our side. I am sure we hit at least three of them through the night, but I never knew what happened to them afterwards.[14]

The capture of the regional command of the National Guard was similar. After being surrounded by tanks and infantry, and given an ultimatum, over one hundred guards handed themselves to the rebels, who gathered the prisoners in the adjacent baseball court for the rest of the night. Additionally, the headquarters of the Carabobo State Police was taken without resistance, as the facility was almost empty at night, being mostly an administrative building.

Minor engagements occurred in multiple parts of the city through the night, as police, *DISIP* and National Guard patrols that were on duty at the time of the uprising were on the loyalist side.

In Fuerte Paramacay, the situation remained tense and immobile for the whole night, with a part of the facility in hands of the rebels and the other in hand of the loyalists, and none of the involved parties daring to attack the other for not knowing what their actual strength was, as well as not knowing what the situation in the city was. The rebels were inferior in number and firepower, being commanded by Captain Carlos Luciano Guyón Celis. To add to the oddity of the situation, there were troop movements between one side and the other, there was not a clear contact line inside the facility.

Forty kilometres south-east of Maracay, in San Juan de los Morros, Hernández Behrens' column was already on the way to Maracay at 00:00 on 4 February. Given the delay caused by the arrival of Flores Tejera, he had to skip the taking of the entirety of Fuerte Conopoima, limiting the rebel activity there to the neutralisation of the gate guards to allow the column to exit.

They joined Godoy Chávez's column in Maracay at approximately 00:40, and together started moving towards Caracas. The group was composed of 32 Scorpion 90 light tanks, and approximately 10 trucks with infantry from San Juan de los Morros, as well as troops from Maracay and Valencia.

Operations in Caracas

In Caracas, the operations of the units headquartered there faced setbacks from the beginning. The *Juan Pablo Ayala* Group had 24 Dragoon 300 IFVs in their inventory, which were divided in two columns that would march towards Miraflores Palace, located approximately six kilometres away, using two different roads. One of the columns was put under command of Lieutenant Jesús Alfonso Elorza Kreubel, who, despite not being a member of the *MBR-200*, expressed support for the operation when the unit was being taken. His column was to depart a few minutes after the first one. However, when the time to start moving came, he headed not towards the presidential palace, but towards General Jorge Tagliaferro de Lima's command; the headquarters of the 3ra *División de Infantería*, still inside of Fuerte Tiuna, at approximately 23:45.

The other half of the vehicles left after being waved out by the sentinels in the northernmost gate of the base. On board were majors Alastre López and Díaz Reyes; captains Aguilera Borjas, Blanco La Cruz, Martínez Rivero, Rojas Suárez and Suárez Montes; and lieutenants Porras Echezuría and Rubén Ávila Ávila; as well as 40 troops from the two rebel-controlled groups.

A team of rebel gunmen being arrested by a member of the National Guard. (Albert Grandolini Collection)

Elorza Kreubel was sent back along with infantry elements of the *Caracas* Battalion to retake the garrisons of both his and the *José Félix Ribas* groups, which they managed to do without facing resistance, as most of the rebel forces had left already, and liberating commanders Contreras Acevedo and Rodríguez Barrios in the process. The members of the two rebel-controlled groups were roaming through Fuerte Tiuna, trying to take various objective buildings. Even though the final plan contemplated that they would try to take over other units and the *AMV*, this part was not executed for unknown reasons, although the most plausible is the state of alert in which the base was placed.

The elements of the *Juan Pablo Ayala* Group that had been tasked with taking the General Command of the Army managed to advance up until the third floor of the building while fighting against elements of the *Daniel Florencio O'Leary* Battalion, which just four hours before had not yet opted out of the operation. Less than 350 meters away, the rest of the unit had joined Aguilarte Gámez's party on its attempt to take the Ministry of Defence, facing the *Caracas* Battalion, which always kept them outside of the perimeter of the building.

Meanwhile, the majority of the *Agustín Codazzi* Regiment went to secure the stretch of the Caracas-Valencia Highway that passes right in front of Fuerte Tiuna, also securing the entrance points of the facility in the process, while the rest of it went to reinforce the two groups that were fighting for the Ministry of Defence and the General Command of the Army.

Loyalist forces were able to keep the *Agustin Codazzi* Regiment at bay, however, preventing them from exiting Fuerte Tiuna or even taking any of the entry points. This was possible because, due to the measures taken as result of the warning sent from General Rangel Rojas' office earlier in the day, fortified positions and more troops had been assigned to the guard posts.

There was still another setback to come for the rebel forces in Fuerte Tiuna. The plan contemplated that a company of 80 men from the *José Leonardo Chirinos* Battalion, commanded by Captain Carlos Guillén Bello, would enter Caracas through the base, assisting in its capture, if it had not been achieved yet; picking up reinforcements; and then marching towards the city centre to participate in the assault of the presidential palace. Shortly after midnight, when the unit reached the southern gate of the complex, upon finding it still under loyalist control, it unexplainably surrendered without fighting, depriving the rebellious forces inside of a much-needed support.

The situation within Fuerte Tiuna progressively got worse for the rebels, who, outnumbered and outpowered, with low resources, and suffering considerable casualties, started to scatter and entrench themselves in different points, most of which would surrender as the hours passed.

The *Antonio Nicolás Briceño* and *José Leonardo Chirinos* battalions left Maracay for Caracas at approximately 21:45, splitting into different columns to avoid losing all forces if the convoy was stopped along the route by the National Guard. During the opening stages of the uprising, Urdaneta Hernández's forces only secured the exit point of Maracay. From there until Caracas, other forces were on their own.

The bulk of the *Antonio Nicolás Briceño* Battalion entered Caracas through the road from Los Teques, while Major Francisco Javier Centeno's men, along with the *24 de junio* Company, did it through the Regional Central Highway, not far away from Fuerte Tiuna. Meanwhile, the *José Leonardo Chirinos* Battalion advanced in a single column, only splitting in multiple smaller convoys when they reached the Tazón toll, in the outskirts of Caracas, approximately at 23:40. Ten minutes later, Francisco Javier Centeno's column passed the same spot.

The bulk of the *José Leonardo Chirinos* Battalion would be personally commanded by Acosta Chirinos and had the task of

A scene in front of Miraflores Palace, with a Dragoon 300VZ armoured car, on the morning of 4 February 1992. (Albert Grandolini Collection)

Yet another Dragoon 300VZ, guarding the main entrance to Miraflores Palace. (Albert Grandolini Collection)

taking the General Command of the *FAV* and the Generalísimo Francisco de Miranda Airbase, both being in the same complex located in the centre of the city, also known as La Carlota. A company, commanded by Captain Miguel Eduardo Rodríguez Torres, had to take La Casona, the official residence of the president. A platoon, led by Sublieutenant Juan Erasmo Valero Centeno, had to take the studios of *Venezolana de Televisión* (*VTV*), and broadcast a prerecorded speech by Hugo Chávez in which he called for other military units to join them in the rebellion, and for the people to stay calm, while also explaining the reasons of the military movement. Finally, there was Guillén Bello's company, whose objectives and fate we have already discussed.

Shortly past midnight, Acosta Chirinos' column reached the airbase. Upon seeing a military convoy approaching, the sentinels opened the main gate and waved them through, only to be disarmed at gunpoint as soon as the paratroopers started to disembark their vehicles. Acosta Chirinos was accompanied by captains Gerardo Alfredo Márquez Reina and Juan Carlos Hidalgo Pandares;

A Dragoon 300 armoured car that crashed through a fence, possibly in the vicinity of Francisco de Miranda Airbase (Albert Grandolini Collection)

lieutenants Eldan Rafael Domínguez Fortty and Pedro Manuel Quiaro Giménez; and sublieutenants José Celestino González and Luis Roberto Arreaza.

Acosta Chirinos and Domínguez Fortty immediately went to the garrison of the *Policía Aérea* of the airbase, thus neutralising the main internal threat. Quiaro Giménez and Celestino González, along with 30 paratroopers, manned the main gate of the airbase and took control of the parking lot of the CCCT Mall, located right in front, and established a defensive position at the southern end of the street. Parallel to the northern perimeter of the airfield, passes the Eastern Highway, one of Caracas' main roads. Hidalgo Pandares set up defensive positions on it to fight any advance of loyalist forces. Finally, Márquez Reina and Roberto Arreaza went to take the General Command of the *FAV*, located in the northern side of the airbase. There, not only the general commander of the Air Force, General Eutimio Fuguet Borregales, had been made prisoner, but also all the force's general staff.

Approximately at 00:30, Lieutenant Ávila Ávila's Dragoon 300 arrived to support the taking of the facility. At the time, the only part of the base that had not yet been taken was the headquarters of the air arm of the National Guard, whose members only surrendered when the building they entrenched themselves into was strafed by the IFV. Before 01:00, the entire base was in the hands of the rebels.

> From my point of view, the taking of La Carlota was the easiest thing we did that day. By using surprise, potential defending forces found themselves surrounded by us before they could even react. I was posted to the checkpoint set up at the northern end of the street that leads to the main gate of the base. Even before the National Guard unit surrendered, many officers from the Army, Air Force and National Guard, started to arrive. All of them were disarmed and taken prisoners and shown the due respect according to their ranks. Through the night, we were harassed by loyalist forces, especially from the National Guard. They did not try to retake the facility, they just surrounded us, I guess because they were aware that we had superior firepower. Shortly after securing the airfield, our officer in charge of communications, Lieutenant José Adelino Ornelas Ferreira, received news from other rebel units, saying that, so far, the operation was successful. This boosted our morale, which was already through the roof.[15]

Loyalist troops deployed in the vicinity of the Museo Histórico Militar. (Albert Grandolini Collection)

Five hundred meters north of the eastern end of the runway is La Casona, which was reached by Rodríguez Torres' men a few minutes later after Acosta Chirinos' made it to La Carlota. Upon arriving, they found more activity than expected, with extra units of both the Presidential Honor Guard and the civilian escort, mostly composed by *DISIP* agents, and the facility on a seemingly lockdown situation. The officer who oversaw the defence of the residency was Lieutenant Colonel Luciano Alfonso José Bacalao von Schambert, who had graduated the *AMV* in the same class as Chávez. Despite the presence of a defending force stronger than anticipated, Rodríguez Torres decided to proceed with the attack.

Members of the National Guard during the siege of La Carlota Air Base. (Albert Grandolini Collection)

One platoon, headed by Lieutenant José Ángel Calatayud Pedra, was tasked with attacking the main gate of the compound, while another two, commanded by sublieutenants Fernando José Cabrera Landaeta and José Alberto Carregal Cruz, attacked the northern and southern flanks, respectively. During the opening minutes of the engagement, the rebels managed to capture eight of the defenders. However, as the attack was already being expected, the initial push was not as successful as had been intended during its planning.

Shortly after the exchange of fire began, loyalist reinforcements started to arrive. Patrols from both the *DISIP*, the Miranda State Police and the *Policía Metropolitana de Caracas* (*PM*, Caracas Metropolitan Police) had a clear view of Rodríguez Torres' positions from the Eastern Highway, but from a point out of sight for Captain Hidalgo Pandares' men, as well as from higher surrounding buildings. The rebels were in a very vulnerable position.

La Casona is located in a densely populated, middle-class neighbourhood of Caracas. It was from there that information about the uprising began to spread first across the city, and then of the country.

The main advantage for defending forces were the high fortified walls of the compound, which the rebels were unable to break despite having used AT4s and rifle grenades. On top of this, was the situation of partial-surrounding in which Rodríguez Torres' forces found themselves as soon as reinforcements started to arrive. The only part of the facility that they managed to capture was the parking lot, which was an open area with only a small building for surveillance on it. Two AFAG gunners were emplaced there, one shooting towards La Casona and one towards the Eastern Highway. However, they were unable to force the loyalists to fall back.

Controversies

Two of the most controversial events of the siege were the deaths of sub lieutenants Cabrera Landaeta and Carregal Cruz. According to the widely accepted version, Carregal was hit in one leg during one of the pushes towards the compound, falling in no-man's land. After some minutes, during a push back by loyalists, he was executed point-blank by a *DISIP* agent who exited the facility. Cabrera's death happened in similar circumstances. His men last saw him alive as they retreated from a small park on the opposite side of the street north of the complex, having been forced out by advancing government forces. He was last seen bandaging some unspecified wounds, covered between two flowerpots. His autopsy, however, revealed multiple point-blank bullet wounds consistent with an execution.[16]

> Earlier in the day, it was decided to double the security detail around the president. We had heard the rumours about the uprising, but we had also heard similar things before, so we did not think much about it. I was on the rooftop of the presidential residency, commanding a group of 30 *DISIP* agents that composed the civilian escort of the head of State. Shortly past 00:15, we saw a group of soldiers arrive, we could tell they were paratroopers because of their red berets, but what caught our attention the most was that they had their faces painted. We didn't shoot first because we did not know exactly why they were there. It didn't take long for the exchange of fire to start, however, after which I immediately asked for reinforcements, and soon after *DISIP* patrols started to arrive. Through the night, and surprisingly, considering how fierce the combat was, there were no deaths

Another platoon from the National Guard (some in civilian attire, others in uniforms) tensely monitoring developments inside La Carlota Air Base. (Albert Grandolini Collection)

Civilians that sided with rebellion being taken out of the studios of *Venezolana de Televisión* by members of the National Guard. (Albert Grandolini Collection)

among the *DISIP* agents that were already in La Casona; only among the reinforcements that came later.[17]

The smallest force of the *José Leonardo Chirinos* Battalion was Valero Centeno's platoon, tasked with occupying the studios of *Venezolana de Televisión*, located less than 900 meters north of the official residency, and transmitting Hugo Chávez's message. However, this could not be accomplished, as the tape he had been provided with was of the U-matic format, not supported by the TV station's equipment, which primarily worked with VHS. The fact that rebel leaders only contemplated transmitting the message through a single channel, and that the task was given to a young officer, demonstrates that they did not give much importance to the media effect for the coup, which was, ultimately, one of the reasons for their failure.

The rest of the column that departed Fuerte Tiuna, now left with only 11 Dragoon 300s, reached Miraflores palace approximately at 00:30. Having split along the road, they approached the compound from two directions, north and south. They were the bulk of the force that attacked the seat of the executive power. Like Rodríguez Torres in La Casona, they found the palace in lockdown, which was already a setback not contemplated during planning. As soon as they arrived, they started being shot at by the defenders.

Using two of the IFVs, the rebels tore down the main gate and entered the compound, followed by infantry, from both the units from Fuerte Tiuna and a company of the *Antonio Nicolás Briceño* Battalion. There were three members of the government in the palace at the time: the president, who had arrived approximately 30 minutes before; Virgilio Ávila Vivas, Minister of Interior; and Luis Alfaro Ucero, senator and Secretary General of *AD*.

Rebel soldiers entered the perimeter and blew up the *Puerta Amarilla* (Yellow Gate), ceremonially exclusively for presidential use, which leads to the anteroom of the president's office, where high-ranking members of the security device were, namely Admiral Mario Iván Carratú Molina and Colonel Rafael Eduardo Hung Díaz, chief and deputy chief, respectively, of the president's security; Lieutenant Colonel Rommel José Fuenmayor León; and Commissar Hernán Antonio Fernández Besembel, of the *DISIP*, chief of the civilian escort of the president.

Fuenmayor León engaged the rebels while the rest fell back into the hallways of the palace along with President Pérez, who at the time had managed to grab an Uzi from one of the defenders, and the other politicians. After approximately 15 minutes, the rebels had succeeded in taking the western half of the building, leaving its central yard as a no-man's land. During this stage of the attack, both Blanco La Cruz and Rojas Suárez sustained serious injuries, and their evacuation forced the attacking forces to fall back from the perimeter of the compound. From that point, and until their eventual surrender, rebels were confined to the street that passes in front of Miraflores.

The company of the *Antonio Nicolás Briceño* Battalion that participated in the taking of the presidential palace was the part of it that was involved in the most action that day. The bulk of the battalion, personally commanded by Chávez Frías went to the *Museo Histórico Militar* (Military History Museum) and its surroundings, located on a hilltop approximately 850 meters west of Miraflores, which could be seen from the rooftop of the building. The compound was reached shortly past midnight. The command post of the operation was set up there, and most of the battalion remained on hold to act as reinforcements if any of the other units requested it.

Another part of the *Antonio Nicolás Briceño* Battalion, a company commanded by lieutenants Freddy Rodríguez González and Wilfredo Figueroa Chacín, was tasked with taking the General Command of the Navy, which they reached at approximately 00:30. This was part of the group that had been sent to the Campo de Carabobo earlier in the day. Figueroa took most of the men and established a perimeter around the compound, while Rodríguez approached the guards watching the main gate and told their commanding officer that he had been ordered to protect the facility because there was a coup d'état going on, and asked to be allowed into it along with his men. Upon receiving a negative answer, the

A Dragoon 300VZ moving in direction of the La Casona. (Albert Grandolini Collection)

Loyalist troops with a Dragoon 300VZ guarding a crossroad near the Museo Histórico Militar, early on 4 February 1992. (Albert Grandolini Collection)

rebels turned their weapons on the guards, who, outnumbered and outpowered, surrendered. From inside of the building, other guards noticed what was happening, and started shooting towards the putschists, injuring Rodríguez González in one hand.

The rebels only managed to control the front yard of the facility, engaging sporadically with the defenders for approximately two hours. AT4s and rifle grenades were fired at the building, hoping to force the loyalists to fall back, but to no avail. Meanwhile, part of the company went to set up a checkpoint one block south of the target, both to take prisoners and to prevent the National Guard, some of whose patrols engaged briefly with the rebels before speeding out, from getting too close to the main force.

Vice Admiral Ignacio Peña Cimarro, general commander of the Navy, barely avoided being captured by making a U-turn and fleeing the scene less than 100 meters away from the checkpoint, while driving towards his office. He contacted the 2do *Batallón de Infantería de Marina Rafael Urdaneta*, in Puerto Cabello, and ordered them to gear-up and remain on hold until further orders were given.

> We only learned that we were going to participate in a coup d'état shortly before we reached the target building. The only ones who

One of several hundred casualties from the fighting of 4 February 1992. (Albert Grandolini Collection)

A *DISIP* agent engaging rebel forces on the streets of Caracas. (Albert Grandolini Collection)

A wounded loyalist soldier being evacuated. (Albert Grandolini Collection)

Members of the National Guard standing next to the body of an unknown soldier: it remains unclear on what side he fought. (Albert Grandolini Collection)

protested were three recently conscripted soldiers, but the rest accepted to participate. We parked our column in the back of the compound and then went by foot towards the front. After a short dialogue between our commander and the chief of the guards, out of nowhere, we started being shot at. Despite having a higher firepower, we were unable to advance, as the defenders had the higher ground, and we lacked enough cover. Multiple times we tried to push towards the building, but we were repelled. A small checkpoint was set up south of our position, and approximately 20 officers, mostly from the Navy, naturally, were made prisoners. We took them to the small surveillance building in the entrance of our target, to prevent defenders from using explosives against us; they were a sort of human shield. We resisted for more than two hours in our position, but at some point, between 02:30 and 03:00, our commander decided that we would abandon our mission and go somewhere else.[18]

Operations in Maracaibo

Maracaibo, like Maracay and Valencia, was taken swiftly by Arias Cárdenas' men. According to Ochoa Antich, the division of tasks was as follows: Major Fernando Viloria Gómez, deputy commander of the *José Gregorio Monagas* Group, would be in charge of the defence of Libertador Barracks; lieutenants Torrealba Machado and Gustavo Barroso Fuenmayor, together with Sublieutenant Eduardo Escalante Pérez, had to take La Chinita International Airport, southwest of the city, which shares the runway with General en Jefe Rafael Urdaneta Airbase, where both *FAV* and National Guard units were based. Lieutenant Oscar José D'Jesús Darnoutt would assault the residence of the governor of the state of Zulia, Oswaldo Álvarez Paz, and take him prisoner. Captain Frang Rafael Morales and Sublieutenant Fernando Prieto Ochoa, Ochoa Antich's nephew, would take the regional command of the National Guard, the 35th Detachment and the local *DISIP* headquarters. Finally, captains Carlos Luis Durante Mariño and José Homero Albarrán Barrios would take charge of public security through the city and the eastern shore of the Maracaibo Lake, each commanding a company for the task.

Frang Morales commanded the only force from Fuerte Mara, the main military base of the city, located in the northern outskirts, that joined the rebellion. He brought a company of the *Francisco Aramendi* Mechanised Group, with several M35 trucks and four TPz Fuchs APCs, and officers among whom was Lieutenant Francisco José Ameliach Orta.

Despite being smaller in number and firepower than anticipated, surprise played in Arias Cárdenas' favour, having been able to capture all targets by 00:30 facing minimal resistance, mostly from the Zulia State Police and *DISIP*.

We left Libertador Barracks at 23:15, approximately. As the column advanced through the city, various of the trucks broke off the formation, heading to their targets. Ours, the *DISIP*

Three members of the National Guard tensely guarding a crossroad. At least two have been issued with ballistic vests, and all are armed with FN/FAL assault rifles. (Albert Grandolini Collection)

A Dragoon 300VZ and loyal troops in front of Miraflores Palace in the aftermath of the coup attempt from 4 February 1992. (Albert Grandolini Collection)

headquarters on the northern end of El Milagro Avenue, was the second-to-last of the convoy that headed north. After that, there was only the regional command of the National Guard. When we got to our target, the agents were already aware of what was happening, and had set up powerful lights pointing towards the avenue, to blind us. As we approached, we were shot at first. I was one of the six soldiers standing on the platform of the truck, and was able to see that they were armed simply with revolvers and handguns. We did a U-turn a few meters ahead, and shot back at them during our second pass. Obviously, our firepower was much higher, having not only FALs, but also an AFAG operator with us. We did two or three more passes, and they surrendered. We disembarked the truck and started heading towards the building. At that moment, two *DISIP* patrols, two Chevrolet Malibu, appeared and were speeding towards us while the occupants shot in our direction. Our AFAG operator shot back, causing the two patrols to lose control and crash. There were four agents in each, all were dead when we went to check, killed either by bullets of by the injuries sustained when their cars flipped several times. There were another four dead agents in the *DISIP* building. After the location was secured, I was sent to the 35th Detachment of the National Guard as part of a reinforcement group. It took us approximately three hours, but they eventually surrendered, right before sunrise. After that, I was sent back to Libertador Barracks.[19]

Arias Cárdenas personally coordinated the attempted taking of the operational command of the *11era Brigada de Infantería*, located less than 500 meters from Libertador Barracks. However, he was unable to do so, as the defenders, numbered approximately 50, entrenched themselves in the building. Not considering this a major setback, he ordered his men to siege it, cutting the electricity and water supply. What he did not know is that inside was General Richard Salazar Rodríguez, chief of staff of the brigade, who alerted General Néstor Rafael Lara Estraño, commander of the *1ra División de Infantería*, to the situation.

The taking of the residence of the governor was achieved without facing resistance, as the guards, agents of the Zulia State Police, surrendered when they found themselves surrounded by members of the Army. Arias Cárdenas went to meet the governor after leaving a part of his men sieging the aforementioned loyalist position. He spent hours in dialogue with Álvarez Paz.

REFERENCES

N/A, 'Hunting Percival (BAC) Jet Provost T.Mk.52', *http://www.fav-club.com*, 20 August 2014

N/A, 'Embraer EMB-312 T-27/AT-27 Tucano', *http://www.fav-club.com*, accessed 28 December 2014

N/A, 'El famoso "teniente Bracamonte" recuerda la sustracción de armas que protagonizó poco después del 4-F | "Está llegando el día de saber quién está y quién no con el chavismo"' *http://www.correodelorinoco.gob.ve*, 15 March 2015

N/A, IAI/Ramta RBY Mk.1., *http://www.fav-club.com*, 30 July 2015

N/A, En fotos: la construcción de las fragatas 'Lupo' clase 'Mariscal Sucre', http://www.fav-club.com, 8 June 2019

N/A., *Proclama de 1902 Ante el Bloqueo Imperialista* (Caracas: Ministerio del Poder Popular del Despacho de la Presidencia de la República Bolivariana de Venezuela, 2015)

Abreu, H., *Frente Guerrillero Manuel Ponte Rodríguez y sus comandantes* (Caracas: Fundación Editorial El Perro y La Rana, 2017)

Andrade, J., *Latin American Military Aviation* (Leicester: Midland Publishing, 1982)

Anselmi, R., *Lo que tengo que contar: Mi vida en tres golpes* (Scotts Valley: CreateSpace, 2017)

Aveledo, G.; Olivar, J., *Cuando las Bayonetas Hablan: Nuevas Miradas Sobre la Dictadura Militar, 1948-1958.* (Caracas: Universidad Metropolitana, 2015)

Azpúrua, C., *4F en la historia* [Documentary] (Caracas: Fundación Villa del Cine, 2012)

Berrizbeitia, A.; Capecchi, F. 'Los Aviones del Benemérito', *http://www.fav-club.com*, 5 February 2014

Betancourt, R.; Romero, A., *Antología Política: 1948-1952* (Caracas: Universidad Central de Venezuela, 1990)

Blanco, J. *Bosquejo Histórico de la Revolución de Venezuela* (Caracas: Academia Nacional de Historia, 1960)

Blanco, A., *La Lucha Armada: Hablan 5 Jefes* (Caracas: Universidad Central de Venezuela, 1980)

Bolívar, M., *El Porteñazo* (Caracas: Fundación Editorial El Perro y La Rana, 2018)

Bracamonte, L., 'La Incorporación del Pueblo a la Nación Venezolana: 1945-1948', *Memorias (11)*, 2009.

Bratzel, J.; Leonard, T., *Latin America During World War II* (Plymouth: Rowman & Littlefield Publishers, 2007)

Buttó, L., 'El Golpismo se Viste de Blanco: Insurrecciones Navales Contra la Naciente Democracia Venezolana', *Tiempo y Espacio (64)*, 2015

Contreras, E., *Del 4 de febrero al 27 de noviembre: habla el general Visconti* (Caracas: Ediciones y Producciones Comuna, 2000)

Daniels, E., *Militares y Democracia: Papel de la Institución Armada de Venezuela en la Consolidación de la Democracia*, (Caracas: José Agustín Catalá, 1992)

Farage, L. February 14th of 2019 'El Mejillón, un Pequeño Héroe al Servicio de Dos Armadas', *http://www.fav-club.com*, 14 February 2019

Fuentes, E., *Síntesis de la Evolución Histórica de las Fuerzas Armadas Venezolanas* (Caracas: Ediciones del Instituto de Previsión Social de las Fuerzas Armadas, 1996)

Gabaldón, E., *Por el camino de Chimiro, con la brigada de los ríos y las filas* (Caracas: Fundación Editorial El Perro y La Rana, 2018)

Gómez, H., *Hugo Chávez, del 4 de febrero a la V República* (Caracas: Fundación Editorial El Perro y La Rana, 2012)

Guevara, I., *Latin American Fighters: A History of Fighter Jets in Service with Latin American Air Arms* (Philadelphia: Casemate Publishers, 2009)

Guía, G., 'Condiciones de vida del soldado: uso y abuso de la tropa en el Ejército Nacional gomecista (1909-1935)', *Conhisremi (3)*, 2007.

Guía, G., 'La Segunda Guerra Mundial en Venezuela y el Apoyo Militar de los Estados Unidos de América a las Fuerzas Armadas Nacionales, 1942-1945', *Mañongo (35)*, 2019.

Harnecker, M., *Hugo Chávez Frías: Un hombre, un pueblo* (San Sebastián: Tercera Prensa, 2002)

Hernández, C., *La Armada de Venezuela en la Segunda Guerra Mundial* (Caracas, Universidad Metropolitana, 2008)

Hernández, C., 'El Transporte de Tropa Blindado Anfibio M-59 en Venezuela', *http://www.fav-club.com*, 21 January 2014

Hernández, C., 'Venezuela en el proceso de "blindar" su espacio aéreo', *http://www.fav-club.com*, 24 November 2014

Hernández, C., 'Venezuela y la Renovación de su Fuerza Submarina, una Asignatura Pendiente', *http://www.fav-club.com*, 13 April 2015

Hernández, C., 'Venezuela y el Fortalecimiento de la Aviación Naval, Otra Asignatura Pendiente', *http://www.fav-club.com*, 20 June 2015

Hernández, C., 'Venezuela, en el camino de fortalecer su aviación de combate', *http://www.fav-club.com*, 9 November 2015

Hernández, C., 'Venezuela, el Fortalecimiento de su Arma de Artillería', *http://www.fav-club.com*, 14 May 2016

Irwin, D.; Micett, I., *Militares y conspiración: De las guerras civiles a los golpes de Estado.* (online publication, 2012)

Jiménez, I., *Venezuela fracturada: Un libro para entender los golpes de Estado* (Caracas: Editorial Dahbar, 2022)

Joquera, J., *Venezuela: The Revolution Unfolding in Latin America* (Sydney: Resistance Books, 2003)

Klaus, E., 'Venezuela Air Force', *http://www.aeroflight.co.uk*, 2007–2012

Lamberg, R., *La Guerrilla en Latinoamérica* (Madrid: Editorial Mediterráneo, 1979)

Linárez, P., *Lucha Armada en Venezuela* (Caracas: Universidad Bolivariana de Venezuela, 2006)

López, D., 'El Dassault Mirage en Venezuela', *http://www.fav-club.com*, 15 January 2014

López, D., 'Dassault Mirage 5V/DV', *http://www.fav-club.com*, 17 June 2014

López, D.; Lugo, J., 'Fuerzas de Operaciones Especiales en Venezuela', *http://www.fav-club.com*, 18 April 2015

López, D., 'El Cazabombardero Ligero VF-5 en la Fuerza Aérea Venezolana', *http://www.fav-club.com*, 19 December 2015

López, D., 'Evolución Histórica de los Vehículos Blindados en Venezuela', http://www.fav-club.com, 13 February 2016

López, D., 'Historia de los misiles aire-aire en la Aviación Militar Venezolana', *http://www.fav-club.com*, 6 August 2020

López, M., *EE. UU. en Venezuela, 1945-1948: Revelaciones de los Archivos Estadounidenses.* (Caracas: Universidad Central de Venezuela, 1996)

Marcano, C., *Hugo Chávez sin uniforme: Una historia personal* (Madrid: Editorial Debate, 2005)

Nieves, P., 'Chávez el 4F: palabras inmortales para la historia', *Cuatro F*, 3 February 2017

Ochoa, F., *Así se rindió Hugo Chávez: la otra historia del 4 de febrero* (Caracas: El Nacional, 2007)
Ojeda, F., *Hacia el poder revolucionario* (Caracas: Fundación Editorial El Perro y La Rana, 2018)
Palacios, A., *4F: Soldados en rebelión* [Documentary] (Caracas: Pana Films, 2012)
Peña Gómez, M., *La Guerra Fría de Venezuela* (Bogotá: Edición Nacional, 1988)
Ramírez, C., *La democracia petrolera: De Rómulo Betancourt a Carlos Andrés Pérez* (Buenos Aires, El Cid Editor, 1978)
Riutort, M.; Balza, R., 'Salario Real, Tipo de Cambio Real y Pobreza en Venezuela: 1975-2000', *Temas de Coyuntura (44)*, 2001
Rivero, M., *La rebelión de los náufragos* (Caracas: Editorial Alfa, 2010)
Sánchez, G., *Hugo Chávez y la resurrección de un pueblo* (Havana: Editorial de Ciencias Sociales, 2014)
Villapol, G., 'El líder del 4F de hoy se llama Nicolás Maduro', *Cuatro F*, 3 February 2017
Visconti, F., *27N: ¡Un golpe aéreo! Capítulo del Proceso Bolivariano Revolucionario* (Unpublished manuscript, 2011)

NOTES

'...y Venezuela siempre será un cuartel'

1 Interview with Captain Ismael Pérez Sira.
2 It was later revealed that the only reason why the *DIM* commander did not go directly to Ferreira was because, being aware of the rumours, he suspected that Ferreira was involved in the plot.
3 Interview with anonymous source no. 2, officer at the 53rd Detachment of the National Guard.
4 Interview with Private Yoel Salazar.
5 Interview with Private Ángel Fernández.
6 Interview with Corporal Néstor Rodríguez.
7 Interview with Corporal Néstor Rodríguez.
8 Interview with Corporal Ángel Méndez.
9 Interview with Private Tierry Parra.
10 Interview with Corporal Simón Borges.
11 Interview with Private Ángel Fernández.
12 Interview with Captain Ismael Pérez Sira.
13 Interview with Corporal Ángel Méndez.
14 Interview with Private José Cordolliani.
15 Interview with Private Carlos Blanco.
16 Interview with Nelson Pacheco.
17 Interview with anonymous source no. 3, part of the civilian escort of the president.
18 Interview with Corporal Luis Peña.
19 Interview with Private Tierry Parra.

Chapter 1

1 Interview with anonymous source no. 1, member of the commission that investigated the first uprising.
2 Interview with Private Tierry Parra.
3 Interview with Captain Ismael Pérez Sira.
4 Interview with Private Omar Espinal.
5 Interview with Private Omar Espinal.
6 Interview with anonymous source no. 2, officer at the 53rd Detachment of the National Guard.

Chapter 2

1 Alternatively, *Alianza Revolucionaria de Militares en Acción* or *Asociación Revolucionaria de Militares Activos* (Revolutionary Alliance of the Military in Action, or, Revolutionary Association of the Active Military, respectively).
2 In 1971, a new academic program was introduced. Among many others, the two main changes it brought about were, on one side, the obligatoriness of a high school diploma for prospective cadets; and, on the other, the inclusion of non-military content, which was divided in three branches: administration, education and engineering. It was with the introduction of this new program that the name of the institution was changed from *Escuela Militar de Venezuela* to *Academia Militar de Venezuela*.
3 The Samán de Güere is an emblematic tree located in the northern state of Aragua that has been linked to a number of transcendent events through Venezuelan history, even since pre-Hispanic times. One such tale mentions that Simón Bolívar rested more than once under the tree.
4 Interview with Captain Ismael Pérez Sira.
5 *Comacate* is the colloquial term used within the Armed Forces to refer to the medium ranks. It is an acronym for *Comandantes, mayores, capitanes y tenientes* (Commanders, majors, captains, and lieutenants). After the 1992 rebellions, it has been used almost exclusively to refer to the specific generation of *comacates* that took part in the events.
6 Interview with Captain Ismael Pérez Sira.
7 Interview with Private Thirone Dávila Ruiz.
8 Interviews with Captain Ismael Pérez Sira and Private Antulio Galvis.
9 At this point, Chávez had managed to position himself as the leader of the *MBR-200*. Earlier that year, on 28 February, Acosta Carlez had been killed during the civil unrest in Caracas and its surroundings. Officially, however, the leadership of the movement was collective; and, indeed, other commanders played key roles in the conspiration, with decisions being taken after discussion among members of the leadership, but Chávez, mainly because of his energic speeches and contacts, was the clear leader. This status was only (indirectly and passively) disputed by Arias Cárdenas, as he was the only one with significant ideological differences with the rest of the leadership.
10 Interviews with Captain Ismael Pérez Sira.

Chapter 3

1 Central Intelligence Agency document number: CIA-RDP79R00967A000200020005-6 (*Venezuela: Caldera and the Military*) dated 17 June 1970.
2 Central Intelligence Agency document number: CIA-RDP03T02547R000100270001-2 (*Venezuela's Policy in Central America and the Caribbean*) dated December 1980.
3 Central Intelligence Agency document number: CIA-RDP86T00608R000500180020-7 (*The Latin American Arms Market*) dated December 1975.
4 Central Intelligence Agency document number: CIA-RDP08C01297R000700060010-0 (*Colombia and Venezuela: Potential for Conflict*) dated 22 February 1971.
5 Central Intelligence Agency document number: CIA-RDP79-00927A005600010002-0 (*Assessment of Latin American Military and Arms Needs*) dated 23 December 1966.
6 Central Intelligence Agency document number: CIA-RDP82-00850R000400070056-9 (*Latin American Report*) dated 27 November 1981.
7 Central Intelligence Agency document number: CIA-RDP79B00457A000700110001-4 (*Arms Sales to the Third World, 1976*) dated September 1977.
8 Renamed *4ta División Blindada* (4th Armoured Division) on 15 December 1995.
9 Central Intelligence Agency document number: CIA-RDP8601017R000505410001-5 (*Will Nicaragua get MiGs?*) dated 24 November 1986.
10 Central Intelligence Agency document number: CIA-RDP85T00176R001300020043-4 (*Implications of the Falklands Conflict for Territorial Disputes in Latin America*) dated 10 August 1982.
11 Central Intelligence Agency document number: CIA-RDP85B00263R000100230008-4 (*An Unconventional Arms Policy: Selling Ourselves Short*) dated 31 July 1983.

12 The Samaritans were never delivered as they were lost in a fire on the ship ferrying them to Venezuela.
13 Central Intelligence Agency document number: CIA-RDP91B00776R000100010031-6 (*Latin America – Warning Meeting – March 1983*) dated 29 March 1983.
14 Central Intelligence Agency document number: CIA-RDP84B01072R000200160024-5 (*Prospects for Stability in the Caribbean Basin Through 1984*) dated 16 April 1982.

Chapter 4

1 Through the presidency of Raúl Leoni, military spending was effectively limited to 10 percent of the national budget, which coincidentally matched the 2.2 percent of the gross national product of the country until 1966. In crude numbers, this means the military spending was approximately 174 million USD during most of the second half of the 1960s.
2 Superior School of the *FAV*.
3 Technical School of the *FAV*.
4 The literal translation of *Cazadores* is hunter, though it is usually used in the military sense to mean light infantry.
5 Central Intelligence Agency document number: CIA-RDP79R00890A001200060014-3 (*Dominican and Venezuelan Forces*), date unknown, but most likely to be from 1963.

Chapter 5

1 Sympathisers of Pérez Jiménez's nationalist views.
2 R. Lamberg, *La Guerrilla en Latinoamérica* (Madrid: Editorial Mediterráneo, 1979) p. 255.
3 *Movimiento 4 de Mayo* (4th May Movement); *Movimiento 2 de Junio* (2nd June Movement); *Unión Cívico-Militar* (Civilian-Military Union); and the various guerrilla groups that were established by members of the *PCV* and *MIR*.
4 F. Ojeda, *Hacia el poder revolucionario* (Caracas: Fundación Editorial El Perro y La Rana, 2018), p. 12.
5 Central Intelligence Agency document number: CIA-RDP73-00475R000201140002-8 (*Venezuela Terrorists Wane*) 31 October 1964.
6 Ojeda, p. 15.

Chapter 6

1 In the beginning, what evolved into the Venezuelan War of Independence was not aimed at creating an independent Republic of Venezuela, but rather to set up a government that would be favourable to the former King of Spain, Fernando VII. The name of the governmental body set up after the events of 19 April 1810, when the people of Caracas ousted the Captain General Vicente Emparán, was *Junta Suprema Conservadora de los Derechos de Fernando VII* (Supreme Junta to Preserve the Fights of Fernando VII).
2 *Afrancesado* (lit. Frenchfied) was the derogatory term used to refer the Spanish officials like Vicente Emparán, suspected of being sympathetic to José I, bother of Napoleon Bonaparte, who had been appointed King of Spain after the Abdications of Bayonne, when Carlos IV and Fernando VII were forced to give up the Crown.
3 *Gocho* is the Venezuelan term to refer the people from the western states of Mérida, Táchira and Trujillo, located in the Andean mountains. From 1899 to 1958, except for the 1945–50 period, the country was ruled by military rulers born in this region.
4 The Battle of Carabobo, fought on 24 June 1821, was the decisive defeat of the Spanish forces in Venezuela. Today, its anniversary is considered one of Venezuela's most important national holidays. The Battle of Las Queseras del Medio, fought on 2 April 1819, saw an unexpected victory by 153 independentist horsemen, led by José Antonio Páez, against 1,200 Spanish riders commanded by Pablo Morillo. In the end, Páez lost only two men, while Morillo lost 400.
5 Also known as Operation *Westindien*.
6 Designations of all Venezuelan warships are prefixed by the abbreviation 'ARV', which stands for *Armada de la República de Venezuela* – Navy of the Republic of Venezuela.

Chapter 7

1 There is no precise English-language equivalent to *caudillo*, though it could be loosely translated to a 'strongman' and/or leader of irregular forces with a regional affiliation.
2 Bolivia, Colombia, Ecuador, Panama and Peru.
3 The period in which the Venezuelan government functioned under the dynamics established during Gómez's rule.
4 Roughly translated as 'The Three Years of the *Adecos*'. *Adecos* being the common name used to refer to the adherents of the *Acción Democrática* Party.
5 M. Riutort & R. Balza, 'Salario Real, Tipo de Cambio Real y Pobreza en Venezuela: 1975-2000', *Temas de Coyuntura (44)*, 2001 p. 10.

About the Author

José Daniel Fernández Dugarte is a Venezuelan-born-and-raised history student in the University of Santiago de Compostela, in north-western Spain. Having been captivated by military history since his childhood, the books on the two Venezuelan coup d'état attempts of 1992 are his first work of this kind.